QUICK & EASY
MICROWAVING ™
SNACKS & APPETIZERS

Developed By The Kitchens Of The MICROWAVE COOKING INSTITUTE ®

Library of Congress Cataloging-in-Publication Data

Quick & Easy Microwaving Snacks & Appetizers.

Includes index. 1. Snack foods. 2. Cookery (Appetizers)
   3. Microwave Cookery. I. Microwave Cooking Institute. II.
   Title: Quick and easy microwaving snacks and appetizers. III.
   Title: Snack & appetizers. IV. Title: Snacks and Appetizers.
TX740.Q52   1987   641.5'882   86-32788
ISBN 0-86573-529-8
ISBN 0-86573-530-1 (pbk.)

Published by Prentice Hall Press
A Division of Simon & Schuster, Inc., New York
ISBN 0-13-749391-6

Contents

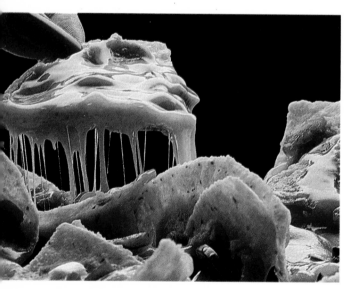

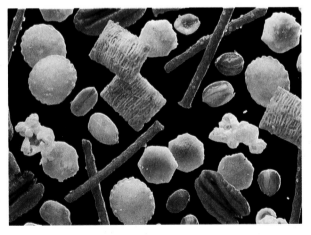

Basic Microwaving for Snacks & Appetizers

*Faster preparation
means more time for recreation*

Everyone likes to enjoy an occasional treat during a relaxing moment, and because those moments are all too few, the ideal snack is one which is quick and easy, as well as delicious.

Welcome to *Quick & Easy Microwaving Snacks & Appetizers,* a collection of fast and fun recipes designed to make your parties more interesting and your leisure time more enjoyable. Almost half of these appetizers can be microwaved in 5 minutes or less.

Create make-ahead appetizers for a formal dinner or cocktail party, enjoy hot snacks during evening leisure time, or leave quick, safe and nutritious snacks for kids to make after school.

Whatever your tastes, *Quick & Easy Microwaving Snacks & Appetizers* may well become the most useful book in your kitchen.

WARMING & SOFTENING CHEESE	
Cheese:	Microwave Time:
Firm aged (½ lb.)	30% (Med. Low) 30-45 seconds
Soft aged (½ lb.)	30% (Med. Low) 15-45 seconds
Cream cheese 3 oz.	High 15-30 seconds
8 oz.	50% (Med.) 1½-3 minutes

Warm up soft or firm cheeses to enhance flavor and make serving easier. Microwave as directed in chart, below. Rotate plate after half the cooking time.

Soften cream cheese in your microwave for easy spreading and quick blending. Microwave as directed in chart, left. *Do not* microwave cream cheese in the foil wrapper.

Line plate with paper towel to absorb excess moisture. Breads don't get soggy and crackers stay crisp.

Restore crisp freshness to stale snacks, like potato chips or pretzels. Place 2 to 3 cups in a napkin-lined, non-metallic basket. Microwave, uncovered, at High for 15 seconds to 1 minute, or until food is warm. Let cool before serving.

Use an ordinary casserole or bowl instead of elaborate fondue or chafing dishes. Return dips or spreads to the microwave for reheating as often as needed.

Save cleanup time — serve appetizers and snacks in the same dish you cook them in. Many appetizers can be cooked on an ordinary serving platter or paper plate.

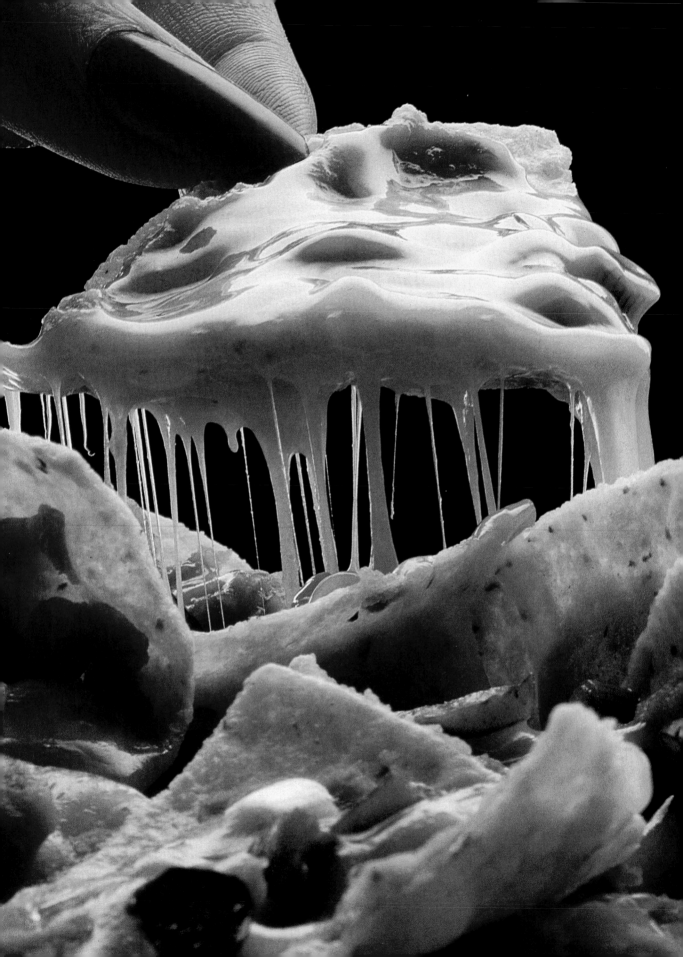

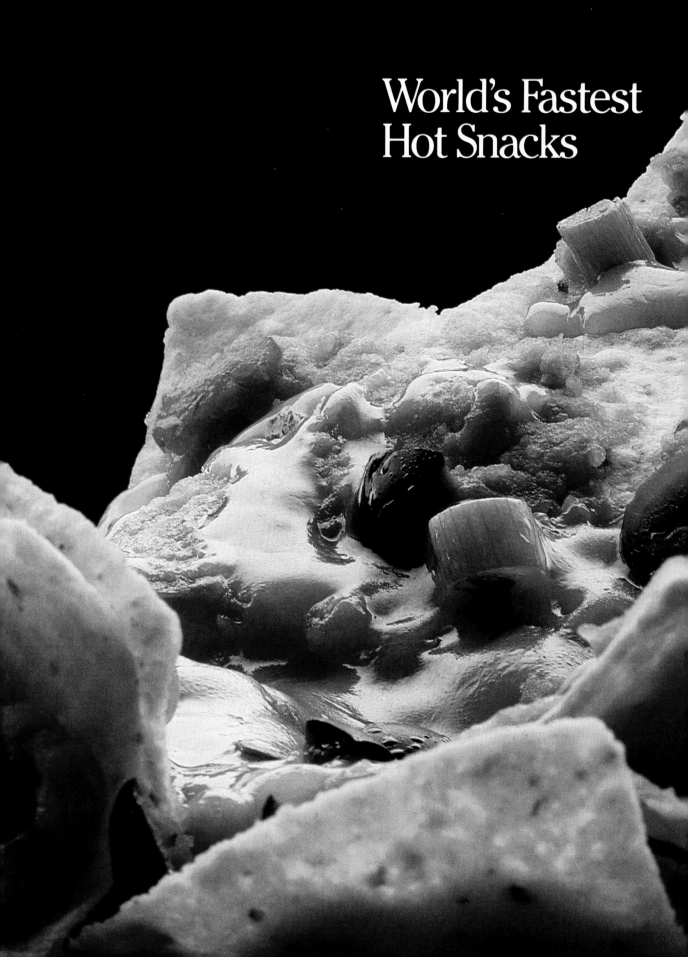

World's Fastest
Hot Snacks

World's Fastest Hot Snacks

Easy enough to make any time...
delicious enough to make often

Nachos Grande (Pictured on pages 6-7)

25 to 30 large tortilla chips
 1 cup refried beans
 1 to 1½ cups shredded Cheddar cheese
 2 tablespoons canned or fresh chopped
   green chilies
¼ cup sliced green onions
 1 to 2 tablespoons chopped black olives

4 servings

Follow photo directions, below.

Total Cooking Time: 1½ to 3½ minutes

How to Microwave Nachos Grande

1 Spread each tortilla chip with 1 heaping teaspoon of refried beans. Arrange 12 to 15 chips in a single layer on a small plate. Sprinkle with some of the cheese, chilies, onions and black olives.

Cracker Snacks ►

4 to 12 assorted crackers
Toppings:
   Shredded cheese
   Pepperoni slices
   Black or pimiento stuffed olive slices
   Cocktail onions
   Anchovies

4 to 12 appetizers

Top each cracker with 1 or more of the toppings. Microwave crackers at High as directed, below.

Total Cooking Time: 20 to 45 seconds

Microwave at High:	Time:
4-6 crackers with topping	20-30 seconds
8-10 crackers with topping	30-40 seconds
12 crackers with topping	35-45 seconds

2 Top with 7 to 9 more tortilla chips, and again sprinkle with some of the topping ingredients. Add the remaining chips and sprinkle with the remaining toppings.

3 Microwave at 70% (Medium High) for 1½ to 3½ minutes, or until the chips are heated and the cheese is melted, rotating the plate 2 or 3 times during cooking.

Variation: Substitute *spicy* refried beans; sprinkle each layer with chopped tomatoes and shredded lettuce; garnish with sour cream and guacamole before serving.

How to Microwave Spicy Cocktail Bites

1 In a 2-quart casserole, combine the barbecue sauce, brown sugar, ginger and cayenne; stir to combine.

2 Add the hot dog pieces; stir to coat. Cover; microwave at High for 10 to 12 minutes, or until the hot dogs are hot, stirring 3 or 4 times during cooking. Serve with wooden picks.

Spicy Cocktail Bites

1½ cups prepared barbecue sauce
2 tablespoons packed brown sugar
½ teaspoon ground ginger
⅛ teaspoon cayenne
1 lb. hot dogs, cut crosswise into quarters

6 to 8 servings

Follow photo directions, opposite.

Total Cooking Time: 10 to 12 minutes

Variations:

Tangy Tomato Bites:
Follow recipe for Spicy Cocktail Bites, except:
Substitute prepared pizza sauce for the barbecue
sauce, and Italian seasoning for the ginger.

Orange Barbecue Cocktail Bites: ➤
Follow recipe for Spicy Cocktail Bites, except:
Butterfly the hot dogs (below); increase barbecue
sauce to 2 cups; omit brown sugar, ginger and
cayenne; add 1 jar (10 oz.) orange marmalade
and ½ teaspoon dry mustard.

How to Butterfly Hot Dogs

Cut hot dogs into quarters. Make shallow
cross-cuts on both flat sides of each piece.
Be careful not to cut all the way through.

Quick Canapés

Four fast & fun party ideas

Ham & Swiss Canapés ▲

> 1 container (8 oz.) Swiss almond cheese food spread
> 1 can (4½ oz.) deviled ham
> 1½ teaspoons freeze-dried chives
> Dash cayenne
> 36 round buttery crackers
> 36 almond slices

36 appetizers

1 In a small bowl, microwave the cheese food spread at High for 30 to 45 seconds, or until softened. Mix in the ham, chives and cayenne.

2 Top each cracker with 1 heaping teaspoon of the cheese mixture and 1 almond slice. (Mixture can also be piped, using a pastry bag and a #6 star tip.)

Total Cooking Time: 30 to 45 seconds

Hawaiian Chicken Canapés ▲

> ¼ cup finely chopped celery
> 1 tablespoon finely chopped onion
> 1 tablespoon butter or margarine
> 1 pkg. (3 oz.) cream cheese with chives
> 1 can (5 oz.) chunk chicken, drained
> ¼ cup drained crushed pineapple
> 2 tablespoons chopped cashews or peanuts
> ¼ teaspoon salt
> 6 slices bread, toasted, trimmed and quartered
> Paprika (optional)

24 appetizers

1 Combine the celery, onion and butter in a medium bowl. Cover; microwave at High for 1½ to 2½ minutes, or until the vegetables are tender. Add the cream cheese.

2 Microwave the mixture at High for 15 to 30 seconds, or until cream cheese is softened. Stir in the chicken, pineapple, cashews and salt.

3 Top each toast quarter with 1 heaping tea-spoon of the chicken mixture. Sprinkle with paprika before serving.

Total Cooking Time: 1¾ to 3 minutes

Chicken-stuffed Zucchini Cups ▲

1 boneless chicken breast half (5 to 6 oz.)
   skin removed
¼ teaspoon dried tarragon leaves
2 thin slices onion
2 tablespoons sliced almonds
1 tablespoon sour cream
1 teaspoon Dijon mustard
¼ teaspoon salt
3 or 4 drops red pepper sauce
2 medium zucchini (each about 8 inches long)
   Shredded carrot (optional)

12 appetizers

1 Place the chicken breast half in a 9-inch round baking dish. Sprinkle with the tarragon; top with the onion. Cover dish with plastic wrap. Microwave at High for 2 to 4 minutes, or until chicken is no longer pink and juices run clear.

2 Finely chop the onions and chicken; place in a small bowl. Stir in the remaining ingredients, except the zucchini and carrot.

3 Cut each zucchini crosswise into 6 equal pieces. Scoop out the center of each zucchini piece with a melon baller, forming a cup. Fill each zucchini cup with chicken mixture. Garnish with shredded carrot.

Total Cooking Time: 2 to 4 minutes

Pizza on a Cracker ▲

36 melba toasts or saltine crackers
1 can (6 oz.) tomato paste
36 slices pepperoni
¾ cup shredded mozzarella cheese
   Dried basil leaves

36 appetizers

1 Arrange 12 crackers on a paper-towel-lined plate. Spread about ½ teaspoon of the tomato paste on each cracker; top each with 1 slice pepperoni and 1 teaspoon of shredded cheese. Sprinkle lightly with basil.

2 Microwave crackers at High for 30 seconds to 1 minute, or until the cheese melts, rotating plate once during cooking time. Repeat with the remaining crackers.

Total Cooking Time: 1½ to 3 minutes

Microwave Tip:
To prevent crackers or toast snacks from becoming soggy, always microwave them on a paper-towel-lined plate.

Party Sandwiches

Bring special flavor to your next party — in 15 minutes or less

◄ Pita Pizza Snacks

    2 whole wheat pita loaves (5-inch diameter)
       split in half, toasted
    ¼ cup prepared spaghetti sauce
    ¼ cup shredded mozzarella cheese
    2 tablespoons chopped green pepper
    ¼ cup sliced fresh mushrooms

                          4 servings

1 Top toasted pita halves evenly with spaghetti sauce, cheese, green pepper and mushrooms.

2 Place pita halves on a paper-towel-lined plate. Microwave at 70% (Medium High) for 1½ to 2 minutes, or until the cheese melts, rotating plate once during cooking time.

Total Cooking Time: 1½ to 2 minutes

◄ Chilito

    1 flour tortilla (6 to 8-inch diameter)
    ⅓ cup shredded Colby, Cheddar or Monterey
       Jack cheese
    2 teaspoons canned or fresh chopped
       green chilies

                          1 serving

Place tortilla on a paper-towel-lined plate, and sprinkle with cheese and chilies. Microwave at 50% (Medium) for 1 to 1¾ minutes, or until the cheese melts, rotating plate once during cooking time. Roll up tortilla, enclosing the filling.

Total Cooking Time: 1 to 1¾ minutes

Salmon Cocktail Toasts

⅓ cup chopped fresh mushrooms
2 tablespoons chopped green pepper
2 tablespoons chopped onion
1 can (6¾ oz.) skinless, boneless salmon, drained
½ cup peeled shredded cucumber
½ cup ricotta cheese
¼ cup grated Parmesan cheese
½ teaspoon Worcestershire sauce
¼ teaspoon dried dill weed
¼ teaspoon seasoned salt
⅛ teaspoon pepper
24 slices cocktail rye bread, toasted
24 thin cucumber slices, cut into halves (optional)

10 to 12 servings

1 Combine the mushrooms, green pepper and onion in a 1-quart casserole. Cover. Microwave at High for 2 to 3 minutes, or until mushrooms are tender, stirring once during cooking time.

2 Add the salmon, shredded cucumber, ricotta and Parmesan cheeses, Worcestershire sauce, dill weed, seasoned salt and pepper. Mix well.

3 Spread about 1 tablespoon of the salmon mixture on each slice of bread; cut each slice in half diagonally. Arrange 24 halves on a paper-towel-lined plate.

4 Microwave toasts at 50% (Medium) for 3 to 5 minutes, or until topping is hot, rearranging slices once during cooking time. Top each half with a cucumber slice before serving. Repeat with remaining toasts.

Total Cooking Time: 8 to 13 minutes

Party Reubens

12 slices cocktail rye bread
   Prepared Thousand Island dressing or
      sandwich spread
 1 pkg. (2½ oz.) sliced, fully cooked pressed
      corned beef
 1 can (8 oz.) sauerkraut, rinsed and drained
 3 slices (¾ oz. each) Swiss cheese, each cut
      into 4 pieces

12 appetizers

1 Toast the bread slices under conventional oven
  broiler. Place 6 toasted slices on a paper-
towel-lined plate. Spread one side of each slice
with a small amount of the dressing.

2 Layer each piece of toast with a slice of
  corned beef, folded to fit toast. Add a generous
teaspoon of sauerkraut and top with 1 piece of
the cheese.

3 Microwave at High for 1½ to 2 minutes, or
  until the sandwiches are hot and cheese
is melted, rotating plate 2 or 3 times during
cooking. Repeat with remaining toast slices.

Total Cooking Time: 3 to 4 minutes

◄ Smoked Cheese & Turkey Salad Sandwiches

 4 slices bacon
 ¼ cup chopped onion
 ¼ cup chopped green pepper
 ¼ cup chopped celery
 1 tablespoon butter or margarine
 2 cups cubed cooked turkey (½-inch cubes)
 ½ cup cubed smoked Cheddar cheese
      (¼-inch cubes)
 ⅓ cup mayonnaise or salad dressing
 1 teaspoon prepared mustard
 1 teaspoon Worcestershire sauce
 4 kaiser rolls (4-inch diameter) unsplit

4 servings

1 Layer 3 paper towels on a plate. Arrange the
  bacon slices on paper towels and cover with
another paper towel. Microwave at High for 3 to
6 minutes, or until bacon is crisp and golden
brown. Crumble bacon; set aside.

2 In a 2-quart casserole, combine the onion,
  green pepper, celery and butter. Cover; microwave at High for 2 to 4 minutes, or until the
vegetables are tender-crisp. Stir in the turkey,
cooked bacon and cheese.

3 Blend mayonnaise, mustard and Worcestershire sauce in a small bowl. Add mayonnaise
mixture to the turkey mixture; mix well.

4 Cut a thin slice from the top of each kaiser
  roll. Scoop out the center of each roll to
within ¼ inch of edge. Fill each roll with ¼
of the turkey mixture.

5 Arrange the rolls on a paper-towel-lined
  platter. Cover with wax paper. Microwave at
50% (Medium) for 3 to 4 minutes, or just until
the cheese begins to melt, rotating platter 3 or
4 times during cooking.

Total Cooking Time: 8 to 14 minutes

Mexican Pizza Sandwiches ➤

2 medium tomatoes, seeded and chopped
¼ cup chopped onion
1 tablespoon canned or fresh chopped
   green chilies
¼ teaspoon garlic powder
¼ teaspoon ground cumin
¼ teaspoon dried oregano leaves
¼ teaspoon salt
3 tablespoons tomato paste
4 slices bread, toasted
1 cup shredded mozzarella cheese

4 servings

1 In a 1-quart casserole, combine the tomatoes, onion, chilies, seasonings and tomato paste. Microwave at High for 9 to 12 minutes, or until the mixture is thick and the flavors are blended, stirring 2 or 3 times during cooking.

2 Arrange toasted bread on a paper-towel-lined plate. Place ¼ of the tomato mixture on each slice of bread. Top each slice with ¼ cup of the cheese. Microwave at High for 1½ to 2 minutes, or until the cheese melts, rotating the plate twice during cooking time.

Total Cooking Time: 10½ to 14 minutes

Vegie Melt Sandwich

1 tablespoon mayonnaise or salad dressing
1 teaspoon prepared mustard
2 slices bread, toasted
2 thin slices red onion
2 thin slices green pepper
2 thin slices tomato
⅔ cup alfalfa sprouts
2 slices (¾ oz. each) Swiss cheese

2 servings

1 Combine mayonnaise and mustard in a small bowl. Spread half of the mixture on each slice of toast. Top each with 1 slice of onion, green pepper and tomato; sprinkle each half evenly with alfalfa sprouts, and top with 1 slice of cheese.

2 Place sandwiches on a paper-towel-lined plate. Microwave at 50% (Medium) for 1½ to 3½ minutes, or until the cheese melts, rotating plate once or twice during cooking time.

Total Cooking Time: 1½ to 3½ minutes

Chicken Pizza Sandwiches

½ cup thinly sliced green pepper
1 small onion, thinly sliced
2 tablespoons olive or vegetable oil
¼ teaspoon crushed red pepper flakes
¼ teaspoon Italian seasoning
⅛ teaspoon garlic powder
⅛ teaspoon fennel seed, crushed (optional)
1 can (8 oz.) tomato sauce
¼ cup sliced black olives
1 cup cut-up cooked chicken
1 cup shredded Cheddar cheese, divided
2 pita loaves (5-inch diameter) split in half, toasted

4 servings

1 In a 2-quart casserole, combine the green pepper, onion, olive oil, pepper flakes, Italian seasoning, garlic powder and fennel. Cover. Microwave at High for 2 to 4 minutes, or until the vegetables are tender, stirring once during cooking time.

2 Stir in the tomato sauce and olives. Microwave at High for 4 to 5 minutes, or until the mixture is hot, stirring once during cooking time. Stir in chicken and ½ cup of the Cheddar cheese.

3 Spoon chicken mixture evenly over the 4 pita halves. Sprinkle with the remaining cheese. Arrange on a paper-towel-lined plate.

4 Microwave sandwiches at 50% (Medium) for 2½ to 4½ minutes, or until the cheese melts, rotating plate once during cooking time.

Total Cooking Time: 8½ to 13½ minutes

Toasting Tip

Toasting breads, muffins or pita halves before microwaving keeps snacks from getting soggy.

Zucchini Pocket Sandwich ▲

1 cup shredded zucchini
½ cup sliced fresh mushrooms
1 cup seeded chopped tomato
½ teaspoon dried basil leaves (optional)
¼ teaspoon garlic salt
3 tablespoons grated Parmesan cheese
4 pita loaves (5-inch diameter)

4 servings

1 Combine the zucchini and mushrooms in a medium bowl. Microwave at High for 2 to 4 minutes, or just until the mushrooms are tender. Drain excess liquid. Stir in tomato, seasonings and cheese.

2 Split open one end of each pita loaf. Divide filling into 4 equal portions, and spoon 1 portion into each pita loaf.

Total Cooking Time: 2 to 4 minutes

Turkey Patty Melts

1 lb. ground fresh turkey
1 tablespoon finely chopped onion
1 tablespoon milk
1 teaspoon Worcestershire sauce
¼ teaspoon salt
¼ teaspoon pepper
⅛ teaspoon garlic powder
4 slices (¾ oz. each) pasteurized process American cheese
4 English muffins, split and toasted

4 servings

1 In a medium bowl, combine the ground turkey, onion, milk, Worcestershire sauce, salt, pepper and garlic powder. Mix well. Divide into 4 equal portions and shape each portion into a 4-inch round patty.

2 Arrange patties on a roasting rack. Microwave at High for 7 to 10 minutes, or until the patties are firm and cooked, turning over once during cooking time.

3 Top patties with cheese slices. Microwave at 50% (Medium) for 2 to 4 minutes, or until the cheese melts. Serve patties in toasted English muffins with catsup or mustard.

Total Cooking Time: 9 to 14 minutes

Dips, Hot & Cold

Bring new taste to crackers, chips or fresh vegetables

Quick Creamy Vegetable Dip

¼ cup hot tap water
1 pkg. (1.4 oz.) vegetable soup and recipe mix
1 pkg. (8 oz.) cream cheese
1 cup sour cream
Dash cayenne (optional)

2 cups

1 In a small bowl, microwave the water at High for 45 seconds to 1 minute, or until boiling. Add the soup mix, stirring to combine. Cover and set aside.

2 In a 1-quart casserole, microwave the cream cheese at 50% (Medium) for 1½ to 3 minutes, or until softened. Add the soup mixture and remaining ingredients; stir to combine. Serve dip with crackers, potato chips and cut-up fresh vegetables.

Total Cooking Time: 2¼ to 4 minutes

◄ Gourmet Dip

1 can (14 oz.) artichoke hearts, drained and chopped
1 cup mayonnaise or salad dressing
½ cup grated Parmesan cheese
⅛ teaspoon garlic powder
Toasted bread crumbs (optional)

2 cups

Combine all ingredients, except bread crumbs, in a 1-quart casserole. Microwave at High for 2 to 2½ minutes, or until the mixture is hot, stirring once or twice during cooking time. Sprinkle with bread crumbs. Serve dip with crackers or cut-up fresh vegetables.

Total Cooking Time: 2 to 2½ minutes

Bacon-Cheese Dip ▲

4 slices bacon, cut into ½-inch pieces
¼ cup chopped onion
1 cup shredded pasteurized process American cheese
1 pkg. (3 oz.) cream cheese, cut into ½-inch cubes
1 tablespoon milk
1 teaspoon prepared horseradish (optional)

¾ cup

1 In a 1-quart casserole, microwave the bacon pieces at High for 2 to 4 minutes, or until almost crisp, stirring once during cooking time. Drain; stir in the onion.

2 Microwave at High for 2 to 3 minutes, or until the onion is tender and the bacon is crisp and golden brown, stirring once during cooking time. Stir in the remaining ingredients.

3 Microwave at 50% (Medium) for 1½ to 3 minutes, or until the cheese melts, stirring once or twice during cooking time. Serve dip with assorted chips and crackers.

Total Cooking Time: 5½ to 10 minutes

Florentine Chicken Dip

- 1 pkg. (10 oz.) frozen chopped spinach
- 2 tablespoons chopped onion
- 1 pkg. (3 oz.) cream cheese
- 1 can (5 oz.) chunk chicken, drained
- ½ cup shredded Swiss cheese
- ¼ cup mayonnaise or salad dressing
- ¼ cup sliced black olives
- ¼ cup milk
- ½ teaspoon salt
- ⅛ teaspoon ground nutmeg
- ⅛ teaspoon fennel seed, crushed (optional)
- ⅛ teaspoon pepper

1½ cups

1 Unwrap spinach; place on a plate. Microwave spinach at High for 4 to 6 minutes, or until defrosted, turning over and breaking apart once during cooking time. Drain, pressing spinach to remove excess moisture. Set aside.

2 In a 1-quart casserole, microwave the onion at High for 45 seconds to 1 minute, or until tender-crisp. Add the cream cheese, chicken, spinach and remaining ingredients; mix well.

3 Microwave at 70% (Medium High) for 2½ to 4 minutes, or until mixture is hot and cheese is melted, stirring once during cooking time. Serve dip with assorted chips or crackers.

Total Cooking Time: 7¼ to 11 minutes

Broccoli Dip ➤

1 pkg. (10 oz.) frozen chopped broccoli
1 small onion, chopped
1 can (10¾ oz.) condensed cream of
    mushroom soup
2 pkgs. (4 oz. each) Neufchâtel garlic cheese
    spread
1 can (4 oz.) sliced mushrooms, drained
1 pkg. (2¾ oz.) sliced almonds
1 teaspoon Worcestershire sauce
½ teaspoon salt
¼ teaspoon pepper
¼ teaspoon red pepper sauce

4 cups

1 Unwrap broccoli and place in a 1½-quart casserole. Add onion; cover. Microwave at High for 4 to 6 minutes, or until the broccoli is defrosted, turning over and breaking apart once during cooking time. Drain.

2 Stir in remaining ingredients. Re-cover. Microwave at 70% (Medium High) for 5 to 6 minutes, or until mixture is hot, stirring 2 or 3 times during cooking. Serve dip with assorted crackers.

Total Cooking Time: 9 to 12 minutes

Variation:

Spinach Dip:
Follow recipe for Broccoli Dip, except: substitute 1 pkg. (10 oz.) frozen chopped spinach for the frozen broccoli.

Serving Tip:
Use hollowed-out fresh vegetables as a colorful alternative to serving dishes. Cut a thin slice from the top of a large green, red or yellow bell pepper. Remove seeds. Cut a very thin, flat slice from the bottom and stand pepper upright. Or hollow out the center of a red, green or savoy cabbage. Spoon in your favorite dip.

Hot Beef, Bacon & Cheese Dip

3 slices bacon
½ cup finely shredded Cheddar cheese
1 pkg. (3 oz.) cream cheese
1 pkg. (2½ oz.) smoked sliced beef, finely
    chopped
2 tablespoons milk
¼ cup sliced green onions

1 cup

1 Arrange the bacon on a roasting rack; cover with a paper towel. Microwave at High for 2½ to 4 minutes, or until bacon is crisp and golden brown. Crumble and place bacon in a small bowl. Stir in remaining ingredients, except onions.

2 Microwave at 70% (Medium High) for 3 to 4 minutes, or until the cheese melts, stirring once during cooking time. Top with onions. Serve dip with assorted crackers.

Total Cooking Time: 5½ to 8 minutes

23

Chicken & Artichoke Dip ➤

1 can (5 oz.) chunk chicken, drained
1 jar (6 oz.) marinated artichoke hearts,
    drained (reserve marinade)
3 tablespoons sliced green onions, divided
¼ teaspoon salt
⅛ teaspoon pepper
½ cup shredded Cheddar cheese
⅓ cup mayonnaise or salad dressing
2 tablespoons plain yogurt or sour cream

1½ cups

Follow photo directions, below.

Total Cooking Time: 2 to 4 minutes

Taste Tip:
For variety or convenience, prepare Chicken &
Artichoke Dip using Monterey Jack or Colby
cheese in place of the Cheddar.

How to Microwave Chicken & Artichoke Dip

1 Combine chicken and reserved marinade in a small bowl. Cover; chill for at least 1 hour. Chop artichoke hearts and set aside.

2 Drain chicken. Stir in the chopped artichoke hearts, 1 tablespoon of the onions, the salt and pepper. Spread mixture over bottom of a shallow 1-quart casserole. Set aside.

Chipped Beef Dip

¼ cup sliced green onions
1 tablespoon butter or margarine
⅛ teaspoon instant minced garlic
1 pkg. (8 oz.) cream cheese
1 pkg. (2½ oz.) smoked sliced beef,
　　finely chopped
¼ cup half-and-half
1 tablespoon lemon juice
2 teaspoons dried parsley flakes
2 teaspoons prepared horseradish

2 cups

1 Combine the green onion, butter and instant minced garlic in a small bowl. Microwave at High for 45 seconds to 1¼ minutes, or until butter melts.

2 Add the cream cheese. Microwave at 50% (Medium) for 1½ to 3 minutes, or until the cream cheese is softened. Mix in the remaining ingredients. Chill for at least 2 hours; serve dip with assorted chips or bread sticks.

Total Cooking Time: 2¼ to 4¼ minutes

3 Combine Cheddar cheese, mayonnaise and yogurt in a small bowl; mix well. Spread mixture evenly over chicken and artichokes.

4 Sprinkle with remaining onions. Cover. Microwave at 50% (Medium) for 2 to 4 minutes, or until mixture is hot. Serve dip with assorted crackers.

Fresh Zucchini Dip

1½ cups shredded zucchini
¼ cup finely chopped onion
¼ cup finely chopped green pepper
1 tablespoon butter or margarine
¾ cup sour cream
¼ cup mayonnaise or salad dressing
1 teaspoon garlic salt
1 teaspoon Worcestershire sauce
Dash cayenne

2 cups

1 Place the shredded zucchini between layers of paper towels. Press to remove any excess moisture. Set aside.

2 Combine the onion, green pepper and butter in a small bowl; cover. Microwave at High for 1 to 3 minutes, or until the onion is tender.

3 Stir in the zucchini and remaining ingredients; mix well. Chill for at least 2 hours. Serve dip with cut-up fresh vegetables or assorted crackers.

Total Cooking Time: 1 to 3 minutes

Hot Artichoke Dip

1 pkg. (8 oz.) cream cheese
1 jar (6 oz.) marinated artichoke hearts, chopped (reserve 1 tablespoon marinade)
⅓ cup sour cream
2 tablespoons sliced green onion
1 tablespoon chopped pimiento
⅛ teaspoon cayenne (optional)

2 cups

1 In a 1-quart casserole, microwave the cream cheese at 50% (Medium) for 1½ to 3 minutes, or until softened. Stir in remaining ingredients.

2 Microwave at 50% (Medium) for 3 to 4 minutes, or until the mixture is heated, stirring twice during cooking time. Serve dip with pretzel sticks or bread sticks.

Total Cooking Time: 4½ to 7 minutes

Curry Dip ▲

1 pkg. (8 oz.) cream cheese
3 tablespoons milk
½ teaspoon curry powder
½ teaspoon garlic salt
1 cup sour cream

2 cups

1 In a small bowl, microwave the cream cheese at 50% (Medium) for 1½ to 3 minutes, or until softened. Blend in the milk, curry powder and garlic salt. Stir in the sour cream.

2 Microwave mixture at 50% (Medium) for 2 to 3 minutes, or until warm, stirring once or twice during cooking time. Serve dip with cut-up fresh vegetables.

Total Cooking Time: 3½ to 6 minutes

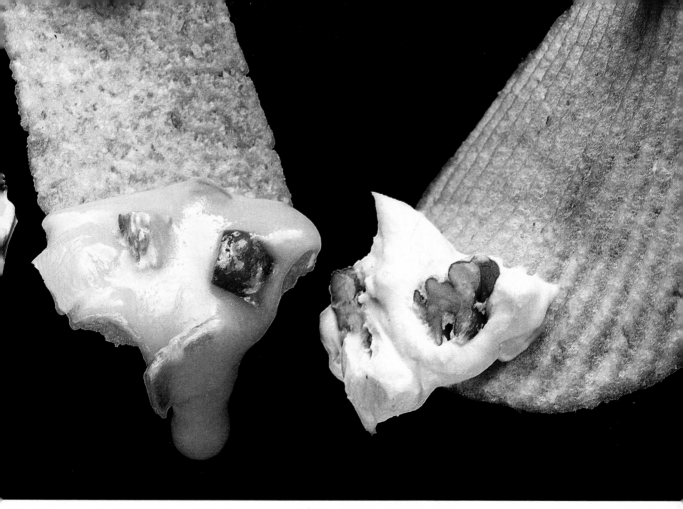

Jalapeño Cheese Dip ▲

½ cup chopped onion
1 tablespoon vegetable oil
2 cups shredded Monterey Jack cheese
2 cups shredded Cheddar cheese
½ cup half-and-half
2 tablespoons canned or fresh chopped
   jalapeño peppers

4 cups

1 Place onion and oil in a 1½-quart casserole;
cover. Microwave at High for 1½ to 3 minutes,
or until the onion is tender.

2 Stir in the remaining ingredients. Microwave at
50% (Medium) for 3 to 6 minutes, or until the
mixture is hot and can be stirred smooth, stirring
2 or 3 times during cooking. Serve dip with tortilla
or corn chips.

Total Cooking Time: 4½ to 9 minutes

Creamy Onion Dip ▲

1 pkg. (8 oz.) cream cheese
¼ cup sour cream or yogurt
1 tablespoon instant minced onion
1 tablespoon water
1 teaspoon instant beef bouillon granules
1 teaspoon Worcestershire sauce
¼ cup chopped pecans

1½ cups

1 In a 1-quart casserole, microwave the cream
cheese at 50% (Medium) for 1½ to 3 minutes,
or until softened. Stir in sour cream; set aside.

2 Combine the minced onion, water, bouillon
and Worcestershire sauce in a small bowl.
Cover with plastic wrap. Microwave mixture at
High for 30 seconds; stir to dissolve bouillon.

3 Stir the bouillon mixture and pecans into the
cream cheese mixture. Serve dip with assorted
chips or cut-up fresh vegetables.

Total Cooking Time: 2 to 3½ minutes

◄ Chunky Salsa

  1 cup chopped onion
 ⅛ teaspoon garlic powder
  1 can (16 oz.) tomatoes, cut up
  1 can (8 oz.) tomato sauce
  1 can (4 oz.) chopped green chilies, drained
  1 teaspoon ground cumin
 ½ teaspoon dried oregano leaves
 ¼ teaspoon crushed red pepper flakes

3 cups

1 Combine the onion and garlic powder in a 2-quart casserole. Cover; microwave at High for 2 to 4 minutes, or until the onion is tender. Stir in the remaining ingredients.

2 Microwave at High for 8 to 11 minutes, or until the mixture is hot and the flavors are blended, stirring twice during cooking time. Chill for at least 4 hours; serve as a dip or sauce.

Total Cooking Time: 10 to 15 minutes

Bean Dip

  1 lb. lean ground beef, crumbled
  1 cup chopped onion, divided
  1 tablespoon chili powder
  1 can (16 oz.) spicy refried beans
 ½ cup catsup
 ¾ teaspoon salt
 ½ cup sliced black olives
 ½ cup shredded sharp Cheddar cheese

5 cups

1 Combine the ground beef, ½ cup of the onion and the chili powder in a 9-inch round baking dish. Microwave at High for 4 to 7 minutes, or until the beef is no longer pink, stirring to break apart once during cooking time.

2 Stir in the refried beans, catsup and salt. Microwave at 50% (Medium) for 7 to 10 minutes, or until the mixture is hot, stirring twice during cooking time.

3 Sprinkle with the remaining onion, the olives and cheese. Microwave at High for 2 to 3 minutes, or until cheese melts, rotating dish once during cooking time. Serve dip with tortilla or corn chips.

Total Cooking Time: 13 to 20 minutes

Mexican Hot Dip ➤

1 lb. lean ground beef, crumbled
1 medium green pepper, chopped
1 pkg. (1.4 oz.) taco seasoning mix
2 cups shredded Cheddar cheese
1 can (16 oz.) refried beans
1 can (8 oz.) tomato sauce
⅓ cup jalapeño relish
   Sliced green onions (optional)
   Sour cream (optional)

5½ cups

1 Combine ground beef, green pepper and taco seasoning mix in a 2-quart casserole. Cover; microwave at High for 4 to 7 minutes, or until the meat is no longer pink, stirring to break apart once or twice during cooking time.

2 Stir in the cheese, beans, tomato sauce and jalapeño relish. Microwave at High for 5 to 9 minutes, or until the mixture is hot and the cheese is melted, stirring twice during cooking time. Garnish with green onions and sour cream. Serve dip with tortilla or corn chips.

Total Cooking Time: 9 to 16 minutes

Chili Con Queso Dip ➤

1 lb. pasteurized process cheese spread loaf, cut into 1-inch cubes
1 can (10¾ oz.) condensed cream of mushroom soup
1 can (4 oz.) chopped green chilies, drained
⅛ teaspoon garlic powder

3½ cups

Combine all ingredients in a 1½-quart casserole; mix well. Microwave at 70% (Medium High) for 8 to 10 minutes, or until cheese melts, stirring 3 or 4 times during cooking. Serve dip with tortilla or corn chips.

Total Cooking Time: 8 to 10 minutes

Rarebit Appetizers

1 can (10¾ oz.) condensed cream of
   mushroom soup
2 tablespoons milk
½ teaspoon onion powder
¼ teaspoon garlic powder
2 cups shredded sharp Cheddar cheese
½ cup shredded pasteurized process
   American cheese
¼ cup white wine

                        2½ cups

1 In a 1½-quart casserole, combine the soup,
milk and seasonings. Microwave at High for 2
to 3 minutes, or until the mixture is very hot but
not boiling, stirring once during cooking time.

2 Stir in the remaining ingredients. Microwave at
High for 2 to 6 minutes, or until the cheese
melts and the mixture is hot and smooth, stirring
after every minute of cooking time. Serve as a
dip with French bread cubes, fresh vegetables or
sliced apples.

Total Cooking Time: 4 to 9 minutes

Spinach Dip Loaf ▲

1 loaf (1 lb.) round sourdough bread
2 pkgs. (10 oz. each) frozen chopped spinach
2 pkgs. (8 oz. each) cream cheese
⅓ cup chopped water chestnuts
3 tablespoons milk
1 teaspoon lemon juice
¼ teaspoon garlic salt
⅛ to ¼ teaspoon ground nutmeg
⅛ teaspoon cayenne (optional)

                        6 to 8 servings

Follow photo directions, right.

Total Cooking Time: 8½ to 12½ minutes

Spinach Dip Tip:
Add one or more of the following ingredients
to prepared Spinach Dip mixture: grated
Parmesan cheese, cooked crumbled bacon,
sliced almonds, chopped hard-cooked eggs,
shredded carrot, pine nuts.

How to Microwave Spinach Dip Loaf

1 Cut a 2-inch slice off top of sourdough loaf. Remove center portion, leaving at least 2 inches of bread on the bottom and 1 inch on the sides. Cut removed bread into cubes.

2 Unwrap the spinach; place on a plate. Microwave at High for 5 to 8 minutes, or until defrosted. Drain spinach, pressing to remove excess moisture.

3 In a medium bowl, microwave the cream cheese at 50% (Medium) for 3½ to 4½ minutes, or until softened. Mix in the spinach and remaining ingredients.

4 Spoon spinach mixture into the hollowed-out loaf. Serve dip with reserved bread cubes, carrot and celery sticks.

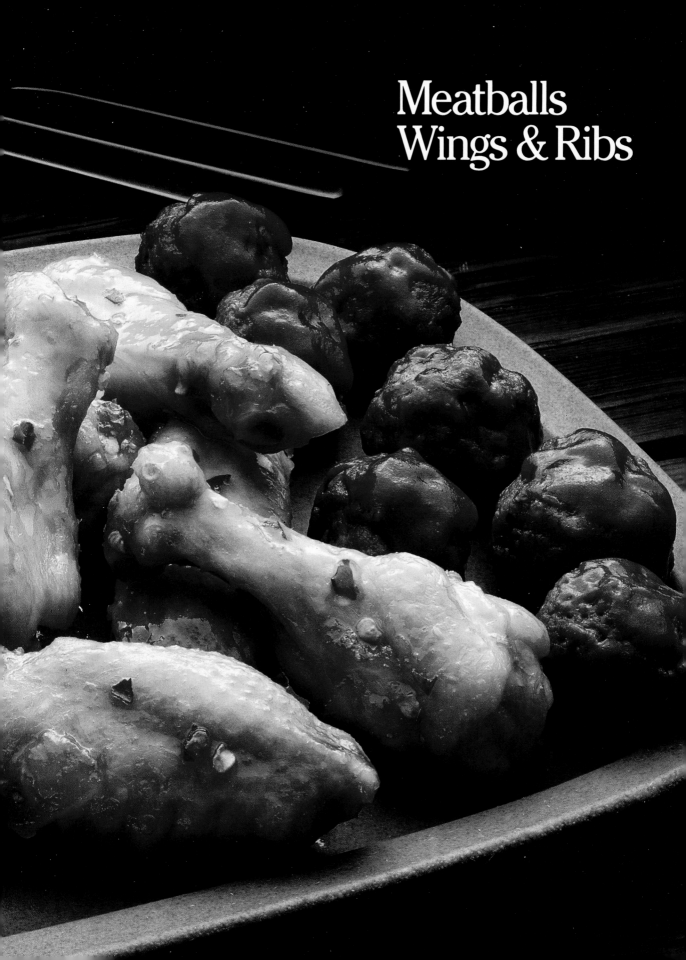

Meatballs
Wings & Ribs

Sherried Meatballs

Meatballs:

⅓ cup unseasoned dry bread crumbs
2 tablespoons milk
1 medium onion, finely chopped
1 tablespoon butter or margarine
1 lb. lean ground beef, crumbled
1 large egg
1 teaspoon salt
¼ teaspoon pepper

Sauce:

Chicken broth or water
1 tablespoon all-purpose flour
¼ cup sherry
1 teaspoon dried parsley flakes (optional)
⅛ to ¼ teaspoon bouquet sauce (optional)

30 meatballs

1 Mix the bread crumbs and milk together in a medium bowl. Set aside. Combine the onion and butter in a 2-quart casserole; cover. Microwave at High for 3 to 5 minutes, or until the onion is tender.

2 Add the onion mixture, ground beef, egg, salt and pepper to the bread crumb mixture; mix well. Shape the mixture into 30 meatballs (about 1¼ inches in diameter). Arrange the meatballs in a 2-quart casserole; cover.

3 Microwave the meatballs at High for 8 to 11 minutes, or until firm and no longer pink in the center, stirring gently to rearrange 3 or 4 times during cooking. Remove meatballs with a slotted spoon; set aside.

4 Drain the cooking liquid into a 1-cup measure. Add enough chicken broth to equal ½ cup of liquid. Blend the broth, flour and sherry together in the casserole. Add the parsley flakes. Microwave at High for 2 to 4 minutes, or until mixture thickens and bubbles, stirring once during cooking time.

5 Stir in the bouquet sauce and add the meatballs. Stir. Microwave at High for 30 seconds to 1 minute, or until the meatballs are hot.

Total Cooking Time: 13½ to 21 minutes

Gingered Meatballs

Meatballs:

1 lb. lean ground beef, crumbled
⅓ cup unseasoned dry bread crumbs
3 green onions, sliced
1 large egg
1 teaspoon ground ginger
½ teaspoon salt
⅛ teaspoon garlic powder

Sauce:

½ cup water
2 teaspoons cornstarch
1 tablespoon soy sauce
2 teaspoons dried parsley flakes
1 teaspoon vinegar

24 meatballs

1 Combine all the meatball ingredients in a medium bowl; mix well. Shape mixture into 24 meatballs (about 1¼ inches in diameter). Arrange meatballs in a 2-quart casserole. Cover.

2 Microwave at High for 5 to 8 minutes, or until the meatballs are firm and no longer pink in the center, stirring gently to rearrange 2 or 3 times during cooking. Remove meatballs and set aside. Reserve the cooking liquid.

3 Combine the water and cornstarch in a 1-cup measure. Blend mixture into reserved cooking liquid in casserole. Add remaining sauce ingredients. Microwave at High for 3 to 6 minutes, or until sauce is clear and thickened, stirring twice during cooking time.

4 Return the meatballs to the casserole, stirring to coat with sauce. Microwave at High for 1 to 3 minutes, or until meatballs are hot.

Total Cooking Time: 9 to 17 minutes

Cocktail Meatballs in Chutney-Chili Sauce

Meatballs:

1 lb. ground beef, crumbled
¼ cup unseasoned dry bread crumbs
1 large egg
1 tablespoon dried parsley flakes
½ teaspoon salt
½ teaspoon chili powder
⅛ teaspoon pepper

Sauce:

½ cup chopped onion
1 tablespoon butter or margarine
1½ teaspoons chili powder
⅛ teaspoon garlic powder
1 can (8 oz.) tomato sauce
½ cup prepared chutney

30 meatballs

1 Combine all the meatball ingredients in a medium bowl; mix well. Shape the mixture into 30 meatballs (about 1¼ inches in diameter). Set aside.

2 Combine the onion, butter, chili powder and garlic powder in a 2-quart casserole. Cover; microwave at High for 2 to 3½ minutes, or until the onion is tender. Add the remaining sauce ingredients; mix well.

3 Add the meatballs, stirring gently to coat with sauce. Re-cover. Microwave at High for 6 to 9 minutes, or until the meatballs are firm and no longer pink in center, stirring gently to rearrange 3 or 4 times during cooking.

Total Cooking Time: 8 to 12½ minutes

Greek Meatballs

Meatballs:

1 lb. ground beef, crumbled
¼ cup chopped onion
1 large egg
2 tablespoons unseasoned dry bread crumbs
2 tablespoons chopped black olives
1 tablespoon dried parsley flakes
1 teaspoon dried oregano leaves
¾ teaspoon salt
¼ teaspoon ground cinnamon
⅛ teaspoon garlic powder

Sauce:

1 can (8 oz.) tomato sauce
1 tablespoon dried parsley flakes

30 meatballs

Follow photo directions, right.

Total Cooking Time: 6 to 9 minutes

1 Combine all the meatball ingredients in a medium bowl; mix well. Shape the mixture into 30 meatballs (about 1¼ inches in diameter).

2 Arrange the meatballs in a 10-inch square baking dish. Blend the sauce ingredients in a 2-cup measure. Pour the sauce over the meatballs; cover with wax paper.

3 Microwave at High for 6 to 9 minutes, or until the meatballs are firm and no longer pink in the center, stirring gently to rearrange 2 or 3 times during cooking.

Hot & Spicy Sausage Balls

Meatballs:
1 pkg. (12 oz.) bulk pork sausage, crumbled
½ cup seasoned dry bread crumbs
¼ cup grated Parmesan cheese
1 large egg
2 tablespoons milk
1 tablespoon dried parsley flakes
⅛ to ¼ teaspoon crushed red pepper flakes

Dipping Sauces:
Prepared sweet & sour sauce
Prepared horseradish sauce
Prepared spicy mustard

25 meatballs

1 Combine all the meatball ingredients in a medium bowl; mix well. Shape mixture into 25 meatballs (about 1¼ inches in diameter).

2 Arrange the meatballs in a 2-quart casserole. Cover, and microwave at High for 6 to 10 minutes, or until the meatballs are firm and no longer pink in the center, stirring gently to rearrange twice during cooking time.

3 Drain the meatballs and serve with one or more of the dipping sauces.

Total Cooking Time: 6 to 10 minutes

◄ Mexican Meatballs

Meatballs:
1 lb. lean ground beef, crumbled
⅓ cup unseasoned dry bread crumbs
¼ cup finely chopped onion
1 large egg
2 tablespoons canned or fresh chopped green chilies
1 tablespoon olive or vegetable oil
1 teaspoon dry mustard
½ teaspoon salt
¼ teaspoon pepper
⅛ teaspoon instant minced garlic

Sauce:
1 can (8 oz.) tomato sauce
1 teaspoon dried parsley flakes
¾ teaspoon chili powder
½ teaspoon sugar
¼ teaspoon ground cumin

36 meatballs

1 Combine all the meatball ingredients in a medium bowl; mix well. Shape mixture into 36 meatballs (about 1¼ inches in diameter). Arrange meatballs in a 2-quart casserole.

2 Blend the sauce ingredients in a small bowl. Pour the sauce over the meatballs; cover with wax paper.

3 Microwave at High for 8 to 11 minutes, or until the meatballs are firm and no longer pink in the center, stirring gently to rearrange twice during cooking time.

Total Cooking Time: 8 to 11 minutes

Serving Tip:
You can microwave meatballs right in the serving dish, and whenever they become too cool, just microwave at High for an additional 1 to 2 minutes to reheat.

Swedish Meatballs ►

Meatballs:
- ¼ cup finely chopped onion
- 1 tablespoon butter or margarine
- 1 lb. ground beef, crumbled
- ⅓ cup unseasoned dry bread crumbs
- ¼ cup milk
- 1 large egg
- ½ teaspoon ground nutmeg
- ½ teaspoon salt
- ¼ teaspoon dried dill weed
- ⅛ teaspoon pepper

Gravy:
- 1 pkg. (1.8 oz.) oxtail soup and recipe mix
- 1¼ cups cold water

48 meatballs

1 Combine the onion and butter in a medium bowl. Cover with plastic wrap; microwave at High for 1 to 2 minutes, or until the onion is tender.

2 Add the remaining meatball ingredients to the onion and butter; mix well. Shape mixture into 48 meatballs (about ¾ inch in diameter). Arrange the meatballs in a 10-inch square casserole. Set aside.

3 Blend the gravy ingredients in a 4-cup measure. Microwave at High for 4 to 6 minutes, or until the mixture thickens and bubbles, stirring 2 or 3 times during cooking. Set aside.

4 Cover meatballs with wax paper. Microwave at High for 5 to 9 minutes, or until the meatballs are firm and no longer pink in the center, stirring gently to rearrange once or twice during cooking time. Drain meatballs.

5 Pour the gravy over the meatballs, stirring to coat. Microwave at High for 30 seconds to 1 minute, or until meatballs are hot.

Total Cooking Time: 10½ to 18 minutes

Barbecued Meatballs

- 1 lb. lean ground beef, crumbled
- ¼ cup seasoned dry bread crumbs
- 1 large egg
- 1 cup prepared barbecue sauce, divided
- 2 teaspoons instant minced onion
- 1 teaspoon dried parsley flakes
- 1 teaspoon lemon juice
- ½ teaspoon salt
- ⅛ teaspoon pepper

36 meatballs

1 In a medium bowl, combine the ground beef, bread crumbs, egg, 1 tablespoon of the barbecue sauce, the onion, parsley, lemon juice, salt and pepper. Mix well. Shape mixture into 36 meatballs (about 1 inch in diameter).

2 Arrange the meatballs in a 2-quart casserole and top with the remaining barbecue sauce. Cover with wax paper. Microwave at High for 6 to 9 minutes, or until meatballs are firm and no longer pink in the center, stirring gently to rearrange once or twice during cooking time.

Total Cooking Time: 6 to 9 minutes

Cinnamon & Spice Chicken Wings

1½ lbs. chicken wings

Marinade:

- 1 can (8 oz.) pineapple chunks
- 1 cup chopped apple
- 1 medium green pepper, cut into 1-inch chunks
- ¼ cup packed brown sugar
- 2 tablespoons raisins
- 1 tablespoon cornstarch
- ½ teaspoon salt
- ½ teaspoon curry powder
- ¼ teaspoon ground cinnamon
- ⅛ teaspoon cayenne

6 servings

1 Separate each chicken wing into 3 parts, cutting at the joints. Discard the wing tips; set chicken pieces aside. Combine all marinade ingredients in a large plastic food-storage bag.

2 Add the chicken wings; secure the bag. Chill for at least 2 hours or overnight, turning bag over once or twice.

3 Pour the chicken wings and marinade into a 9-inch square baking dish; cover with wax paper. Microwave chicken at High for 11 to 13 minutes, or until the meat is no longer pink and the green pepper is tender, stirring once or twice during cooking time.

Total Cooking Time: 11 to 13 minutes

How to Divide Chicken Wings

Cut chicken wings into 3 parts at the joints. Discard the wing tips.

Sweet & Tangy Chicken Wings ▲

1½ lbs. chicken wings

Marinade:

- ¼ cup white wine vinegar
- ¼ cup honey
- 1 tablespoon soy sauce
- 1 tablespoon catsup
- ½ teaspoon ground ginger
- ½ teaspoon bouquet sauce (optional)
- 1 can (8 oz.) pineapple chunks, drained

6 servings

1 Separate each chicken wing into 3 parts, cutting at the joints. Discard the wing tips; set chicken pieces aside. Combine the marinade ingredients in a 2-cup measure. Microwave at High for 1 to 2 minutes, or until hot. Let marinade cool slightly.

2 Combine chicken wings, marinade and pineapple in a large plastic food-storage bag. Secure the bag; chill for at least 2 hours, or overnight.

3 Pour chicken wings and marinade into a 9-inch square baking dish. Cover with wax paper. Microwave chicken at High for 11 to 13 minutes, or until the meat is no longer pink, stirring once or twice during cooking time.

Total Cooking Time: 12 to 15 minutes

Spicy Mexican Chicken Wings

1½ lbs. chicken wings

Marinade:

　1　small onion, finely chopped
　3　tablespoons soy sauce
　2　tablespoons water
　2　tablespoons lime juice
　1　tablespoon packed brown sugar
　1　to 1½ teaspoons Mexican seasoning
　½　teaspoon salt
　⅛　teaspoon instant minced garlic

6 servings

1 Separate each chicken wing into 3 parts, cutting at the joints. Discard wing tips; set chicken pieces aside. Combine all marinade ingredients in a large plastic food-storage bag. Add the chicken wings. Secure the bag; chill for at least 4 hours, or overnight. Drain.

2 Arrange the chicken wings in a 9-inch square baking dish. Cover dish with wax paper. Microwave at High for 7 to 11 minutes, or until the meat is no longer pink, stirring once or twice during cooking time.

Total Cooking Time: 7 to 11 minutes

Polynesian Chicken Wings

1½ lbs. chicken wings

Marinade:

½ cup teriyaki sauce
¼ cup apricot preserves
2 teaspoons lemon juice
¼ teaspoon crushed red pepper flakes
¼ teaspoon dry mustard

6 servings

1 Separate each chicken wing into 3 parts, cutting at the joints. Discard the wing tips; set chicken pieces aside. Combine the marinade ingredients in a 2-cup measure. Microwave at High for 1 to 2 minutes, or until marinade is hot. Let marinade cool slightly.

2 Combine the chicken wings and marinade in a large plastic food-storage bag. Secure the bag and chill for at least 2 hours, or overnight.

3 Pour chicken and marinade into a 9-inch square baking dish; cover with wax paper. Microwave chicken at High for 11 to 13 minutes, or until meat is no longer pink, stirring once or twice during cooking time.

Total Cooking Time: 12 to 15 minutes

Orange-Barbecue Riblets ▲

1½ lbs. lamb riblets
⅛ teaspoon pepper
¼ cup orange juice, divided
¼ cup catsup
2 tablespoons chopped onion
2 tablespoons packed brown sugar
2 teaspoons vinegar
½ teaspoon Worcestershire sauce
¼ teaspoon salt
⅛ teaspoon garlic powder
1 or 2 drops liquid smoke flavoring

4 servings

1 Arrange the riblets in a 9-inch square baking dish. Sprinkle with the pepper and 2 tablespoons of the orange juice. Cover. Microwave at High for 5 to 8 minutes, or until the riblets are no longer pink, rearranging once during cooking time. Drain.

2 Arrange the riblets on a roasting rack. Mix the remaining orange juice and the remaining ingredients in a small bowl. Brush the riblets with half of the sauce.

3 Microwave at 50% (Medium) for 8 to 13 minutes, or until the riblets are tender, turning over and brushing with the remaining sauce once during cooking time.

Total Cooking Time: 13 to 21 minutes

Cocktail Ribs

Ribs:

3 lbs. pork spareribs, cut in half across the bones, then into single rib pieces
⅓ cup hot tap water
1 medium onion, thinly sliced
4 thin slices lemon
1 teaspoon salt
¼ teaspoon dried marjoram leaves

Sauce:

1 cup catsup
¼ cup honey
3 tablespoons chili sauce
2 tablespoons soy sauce
⅛ teaspoon garlic powder
Dash cayenne

12 to 15 appetizers

1 Place the ribs in a 3-quart casserole. Top with the remaining rib ingredients. Cover; microwave at High for 5 minutes.

2 Microwave at 50% (Medium) for 40 to 50 minutes longer, or until ribs are fork-tender, stirring to rearrange twice during cooking time. Let ribs stand, covered, for 10 minutes. Remove the ribs from the cooking liquid and place in a 9-inch square baking dish.

3 Combine the sauce ingredients in a small bowl; pour the sauce over the ribs. Microwave at 50% (Medium) for 5 to 10 minutes, or until ribs and sauce are hot, rearranging ribs once during cooking time.

Total Cooking Time: 50 to 65 minutes

Spicy Pineapple-glazed Ribs ▲

Ribs:

- 3 lbs. pork spareribs, cut in half across bones, then into single rib pieces
- ⅓ cup hot tap water
- 1 medium onion, thinly sliced
- 4 thin slices lemon
- 1 teaspoon salt

Sauce:

- 1 jar (10 oz.) pineapple preserves
- 1 can (8 oz.) pineapple chunks, drained
- ½ cup prepared steak sauce
- ½ teaspoon chili powder

12 to 15 appetizers

1 Place the ribs in a 3-quart casserole. Top with the remaining rib ingredients. Cover; microwave at High for 5 minutes.

2 Microwave at 50% (Medium) for 40 to 50 minutes longer, or until ribs are fork-tender, stirring to rearrange twice during cooking time. Let stand, covered, for 10 minutes. Remove ribs from the cooking liquid and place in a 9-inch square baking dish. Set aside.

3 Combine sauce ingredients in a small bowl; pour sauce over ribs. Microwave ribs at 50% (Medium) for 5 to 10 minutes, or until ribs and sauce are hot, rearranging ribs once during cooking time.

Total Cooking Time: 50 to 65 minutes

Snappy Glazed Ribs

Ribs:

- 3 lbs. pork spareribs, cut in half across bones, then into single rib pieces
- ⅓ cup hot tap water
- 4 thin slices lemon
- 1 stalk celery, cut into 1-inch pieces
- 1 teaspoon salt

Sauce:

- 1 jar (10 oz.) currant jelly
- ½ cup chili sauce
- ⅛ teaspoon cayenne

12 to 15 appetizers

1 Place ribs in a 3-quart casserole. Top with remaining rib ingredients. Cover; microwave at High for 5 minutes.

2 Microwave at 50% (Medium) for 40 to 50 minutes longer, or until ribs are fork-tender, stirring to rearrange twice during cooking time. Let stand, covered, for 10 minutes. Remove ribs from liquid and place in a 9-inch square baking dish. Set aside.

3 Combine the sauce ingredients in a small bowl. Microwave at High for 1 to 2 minutes, or until jelly melts, stirring once during cooking time. Pour sauce over ribs. Microwave at 50% (Medium) for 5 to 10 minutes longer, or until ribs and sauce are hot, rearranging ribs once during cooking time.

Total Cooking Time: 51 to 67 minutes

Seafood Sampler

Seafood Sampler

Light & delightful recipes to highlight your party buffet

Your get-togethers take on a special flavor with these unique seafood appetizers. Microwaving brings out the natural texture and delicate taste of seafoods. Use lower power levels and check frequently to avoid overcooking.

Spicy Shrimp

1 pkg. (12 oz.) frozen small shrimp (uncooked) peeled and deveined
¼ cup white wine
1 tablespoon vegetable oil
½ teaspoon dried parsley flakes
⅛ teaspoon salt
⅛ teaspoon pepper
⅛ teaspoon dried tarragon leaves (optional)
⅛ teaspoon instant minced garlic
⅛ teaspoon crushed red pepper flakes (optional)

6 to 8 servings

1 Place the frozen shrimp in a 9-inch square baking dish. Microwave at 50% (Medium) for 3 to 6 minutes, or until the shrimp are cold but not icy, separating as soon as possible and stirring 2 or 3 times during cooking. Rinse shrimp under cold water; drain.

2 Combine the shrimp and the remaining ingredients in a 1½-quart casserole. Cover with wax paper; microwave at 50% (Medium) for 7 to 11 minutes, or until the shrimp are firm and opaque, stirring twice during cooking time. Let shrimp stand for 2 to 3 minutes. Serve shrimp with wooden picks.

Total Cooking Time: 10 to 17 minutes

Garlic Shrimp

¼ cup butter or margarine
¼ to ½ teaspoon garlic powder
2 teaspoons dried parsley flakes
1 lb. large uncooked shrimp, peeled and
   deveined

6 to 8 servings

Follow photo directions, below.

Total Cooking Time: 6¼ to 9½ minutes

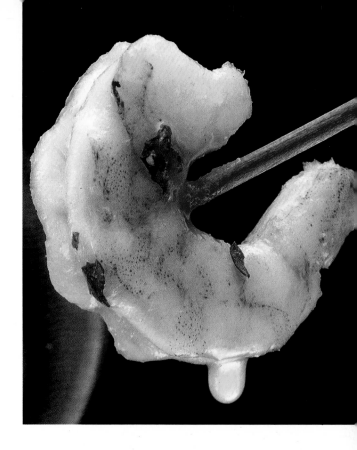

How to Microwave Garlic Shrimp

1 Combine butter, garlic powder and parsley flakes in a small bowl. Microwave at High for 1¼ to 1½ minutes, or until butter melts. Place shrimp in a 9-inch round baking dish.

2 Pour butter mixture evenly over shrimp; cover with plastic wrap. Microwave at 70% (Medium High) for 5 to 8 minutes, or until shrimp are firm and opaque, stirring 3 or 4 times during cooking. Serve shrimp with wooden picks.

49

Shrimp Wrap-ups

    8 slices bacon
    16 medium uncooked shrimp, peeled and
       deveined
    1 small green pepper, cut into 16 chunks
    2 tablespoons soy sauce
    2 tablespoons white wine
    2 tablespoons chili sauce
    2 tablespoons plum or grape jelly

16 appetizers

1 Layer 3 paper towels on a plate. Arrange 4 bacon slices on the paper towels; top with 3 more paper towels and the remaining bacon. Cover with 1 paper towel. Microwave at High for 3½ to 5 minutes, or just until the bacon is slightly cooked.

2 Cut each bacon slice in half crosswise. Wrap one shrimp and one green pepper chunk in each bacon piece. Secure with wooden picks. In a 9-inch square baking dish, arrange the wrap-ups in a single layer. Set aside.

3 In a 2-cup measure, combine the remaining ingredients. Microwave at High for 30 seconds to 1 minute, or until the jelly melts, stirring once during cooking time. Pour the mixture over the wrap-ups; cover and chill for at least 2 hours, turning pieces over once.

4 Arrange the wrap-ups on a roasting rack. Microwave at High for 3 to 4 minutes, or until the shrimp are firm and opaque, rotating rack once or twice during cooking time.

Total Cooking Time: 7 to 10 minutes

50

Seafood-stuffed Brie

1 pkg. (8 oz.) Brie cheese
2 tablespoons chopped pecans
1 tablespoon butter or margarine
1 can (4¼ oz.) small shrimp, rinsed and
  drained
½ cup finely shredded Colby cheese

6 to 8 servings

1 Cut the Brie cheese in half crosswise. Place the bottom half, cut-side-up, on a serving plate. Trim crust from top of the remaining half. Discard crust; set cheese aside.

2 Combine the pecans and butter in a small bowl. Microwave at High for 2½ to 3 minutes, or until the pecans are toasted, stirring after every minute of cooking time.

3 In a small bowl, mash the shrimp with a fork. Stir in the pecans and the Colby cheese. Press half of the shrimp mixture onto the bottom half of Brie. Cover with the top half, and press the remaining shrimp mixture onto the Brie.

4 Microwave at 50% (Medium) for 2 to 2½ minutes, or until the Brie is warm and softened, rotating plate after every minute of cooking time. Serve Brie as a spread with assorted crackers.

Total Cooking Time: 4½ to 5½ minutes

Savory Stuffed Shrimp

8 to 10 extra-large uncooked shrimp (1 lb.)
   in the shells
⅓ cup chopped celery
1 tablespoon finely chopped onion
¼ cup butter or margarine, divided
⅔ cup finely crushed round buttery crackers
1 tablespoon chopped pimiento (optional)
½ teaspoon grated lemon peel (optional)
⅛ teaspoon garlic salt
5 or 6 drops red pepper sauce

                        8 to 10 appetizers

Follow photo directions, right.

Total Cooking Time: 10¼ to 14½ minutes

How to Microwave Savory Stuffed Shrimp

1 Clean shrimp by loosening the shell from the leg side. Carefully peel shell away, leaving tail intact. Make a shallow slit down the middle of the back from tail to thick end.

2 Loosen and remove the vein of each shrimp. To butterfly, slit undersides open from tail to thick end, being careful not to cut through. Flatten thick ends. Arrange shrimp cut-sides-up on a plate, with tail portions toward center. Set aside.

3 Combine the celery, onion and 2 tablespoons of the butter in a small bowl. Microwave at High for 1½ to 2½ minutes, or until vegetables are tender, stirring once during cooking time. Stir in remaining ingredients, except reserved butter.

4 Spoon stuffing evenly onto shrimp, pressing lightly. Cover with wax paper. Microwave at 50% (Medium) for 8 to 11 minutes, or until the shrimp are firm and opaque, rotating plate twice during cooking time.

5 In a small bowl, microwave remaining 2 tablespoons of butter at High for 45 seconds to 1 minute, or until melted. Drizzle butter over the shrimp.

Cajun Shrimp & Scallops

Crumb Topping:

- 1 tablespoon butter or margarine
- ¼ cup unseasoned dry bread crumbs
- ⅛ teaspoon pepper
  Dash cayenne

- ½ cup chopped green pepper
- ¼ cup sliced green onions
- ¼ teaspoon dry mustard
- ¼ teaspoon chili powder
- ⅛ teaspoon dried thyme leaves
- ⅛ teaspoon garlic powder
- 1 can (8 oz.) tomato sauce
- ½ lb. medium uncooked shrimp, peeled and deveined
- ¼ lb. bay scallops
- ¼ teaspoon salt
- ¼ teaspoon sugar

4 servings

1 In a small bowl, microwave the butter at High for 45 seconds to 1 minute, or until melted. Stir in remaining topping ingredients; set aside.

2 In a 1-quart casserole, combine the green pepper, onions, mustard, chili powder, thyme and garlic powder. Cover; microwave at High for 2 to 4 minutes, or until the vegetables are tender, stirring once during cooking time.

3 Stir in the remaining ingredients. Spoon the mixture evenly into 4 individual casseroles or large soup bowls.

4 Microwave at 70% (Medium High) for 8 to 13 minutes, or until the shrimp and scallops are firm and opaque, rearranging twice during cooking time. Sprinkle evenly with the crumb topping during the last minute of cooking time.

Total Cooking Time: 10¾ to 18 minutes

Doneness Tip:
Microwave scallops and shrimp at reduced power levels, just until firm and opaque. If they seem slightly underdone, add 5 minutes standing time before serving.

Scallop-stuffed Mushrooms

⅓ cup sherry
 2 tablespoons sliced green onion
 1 teaspoon olive or vegetable oil
¼ teaspoon dried thyme leaves
⅛ teaspoon garlic powder
 1 tablespoon butter or margarine
⅓ cup seasoned dry bread crumbs
 1 tablespoon snipped fresh parsley
36 bay scallops (½ lb.)
36 fresh mushrooms (1 lb.) stems removed

36 appetizers

1 In a small bowl, combine the sherry, onion, oil, thyme and garlic powder. Cover; microwave at High for 1½ to 2 minutes, or until the mixture boils. Set aside.

2 In a small bowl, microwave the butter at High for 45 seconds to 1 minute, or until melted. Stir in the bread crumbs and the parsley. Cover; set aside.

3 Add scallops to the sherry mixture. Toss to coat. Cover; chill for 1 to 2 hours. Drain.

4 Place 1 scallop in center of each mushroom cap; sprinkle the stuffed mushrooms with the bread crumb mixture, pressing lightly to coat. Arrange ½ of the mushrooms on a paper-towel-lined plate. Cover with a paper towel.

5 Microwave at 50% (Medium) for 2½ to 5 minutes, or until scallops are firm and opaque, rotating plate after every minute of cooking time. Repeat with the remaining stuffed mushrooms.

Total Cooking Time: 7¼ to 13 minutes

Clam Cracker Spread

3 tablespoons butter or margarine
1 medium onion, chopped
½ medium green pepper, chopped
1 teaspoon dried oregano leaves
1 teaspoon dried parsley flakes
⅛ to ¼ teaspoon crushed red pepper flakes
⅛ teaspoon instant minced garlic
2 cans (6½ oz. each) minced clams, drained (reserve liquid)
1 tablespoon lemon juice
½ cup seasoned dry bread crumbs
¼ cup grated fresh Parmesan or Romano cheese

1 cup

1 In a 9-inch pie plate, combine the butter, onion, green pepper, oregano, parsley, pepper flakes and garlic. Microwave at High for 4 to 6 minutes, or until the vegetables are tender, stirring once during cooking time. Stir in the clams, lemon juice and bread crumbs.

2 Stir in the reserved liquid, 1 tablespoon at a time, until mixture reaches desired spreading consistency. Sprinkle with grated cheese.

3 Microwave at 70% (Medium High) for 3 to 4 minutes, or until mixture is hot and the cheese is melted, rotating plate once or twice during cooking time. Serve with assorted crackers.

Total Cooking Time: 7 to 10 minutes

Crab Meat Rounds ▲

2 cans (6 oz. each) crab meat, drained and rinsed, cartilage removed
½ cup sliced green onions
⅓ cup mayonnaise or salad dressing
2 tablespoons snipped fresh parsley
½ cup finely shredded Cheddar cheese
36 melba toast rounds
Paprika (optional)

36 appetizers

1 In a small bowl, combine the crab meat, onions, mayonnaise and parsley; mix well. Stir in the cheese.

2 Spoon half of the crab mixture evenly onto 18 of the toast rounds. Arrange toast rounds on a paper-towel-lined plate.

3 Microwave at High for 1½ to 3 minutes, or until the crab mixture is hot and cheese is melted, rotating plate once or twice during cooking time. Repeat with remaining mixture. Sprinkle with paprika before serving.

Total Cooking Time: 3 to 6 minutes

Smoked Oyster Dip

2 tablespoons finely chopped celery
1 tablespoon finely chopped onion
2 teaspoons butter or margarine
½ cup sour cream or plain yogurt
1 can (3½ oz.) smoked oysters, drained and
   coarsely chopped
2 tablespoons mayonnaise or salad dressing
1 tablespoon snipped fresh parsley
2 teaspoons lemon juice
¼ teaspoon freshly ground pepper

                    1 cup

Combine the celery, onion and butter in a small bowl. Cover with plastic wrap; microwave at High for 1 to 2½ minutes, or until the vegetables are tender-crisp. Stir in the remaining ingredients. Chill for at least 1 hour. Serve dip with assorted cut-up fresh vegetables.

Total Cooking Time: 1 to 2½ minutes

Spreads & Pâtés

Spreads & Pâtés

Versatile, easy & elegant — perfect for quiet snacking or formal entertaining

Port Wine Cheese Apple (opposite)

- 1 pkg. (3 oz.) cream cheese
- 1½ cups finely shredded Cheddar cheese
- 1 tablespoon port wine
  Paprika
- 1 cinnamon stick
- 1 bay leaf

4 to 6 servings

1 In a medium bowl, microwave the cream cheese at High for 15 to 30 seconds, or until softened. Blend in the Cheddar cheese and port wine. Wrap the cheese mixture in a sheet of plastic wrap and shape into a ball. Chill for about 1 hour, or until ball is slightly set.

2 Form wrapped cheese ball into the shape of an apple. Unwrap; sprinkle with paprika. Use the cinnamon stick to form the stem, and the bay leaf for the apple leaf. Serve cheese ball with assorted crackers, apple and pear slices, or grape clusters.

Total Cooking Time: 15 to 30 seconds

Holiday Cheeses. Be creative! Mold cheese mixture into the shape of a Christmas tree, Halloween pumpkin or a Valentine's heart. Try different garnishes and coatings.

Holiday Cheese Ball
(pictured on pages 58-59)

- ¼ cup chopped green pepper
- ¼ cup sliced green onions
- 1 teaspoon butter or margarine
- 1 pkg. (8 oz.) cream cheese
- 2 cups shredded Cheddar cheese
- 1 pkg. (4 oz.) blue cheese, crumbled
- 1 tablespoon chopped pimiento
- 2 teaspoons prepared horseradish
- 2 teaspoons Worcestershire sauce
- ⅛ teaspoon garlic powder
- ½ cup chopped pecans

10 to 12 servings

1 Combine the green pepper, onion and butter in a small bowl. Cover; microwave at High for 30 seconds to 1 minute, or until the vegetables are tender-crisp. Set aside.

2 In a large bowl, microwave the cream cheese at 50% (Medium) for 1½ to 3 minutes, or until softened. Stir in the vegetables and the remaining ingredients, except the pecans. Wrap the cheese mixture in a sheet of plastic wrap and shape into a ball. Chill for 2 to 3 hours.

3 Unwrap and roll the cheese ball in the chopped pecans. Serve cheese ball with assorted crackers.

Total Cooking Time: 2 to 4 minutes

Easy Layered Cheese Loaf ➤

4 oz. cream cheese
2 tablespoons butter or margarine
½ teaspoon dried basil leaves
3 slices (¾ oz. each) Colby cheese
3 slices (¾ oz. each) brick cheese
1 slice (¾ oz.) salami
2 tablespoons snipped fresh parsley

1 cheese loaf

1 In a small bowl, microwave the cream cheese and the butter at 30% (Medium Low) for 30 seconds to 1½ minutes, or until the mixture is softened, rotating bowl after every 15 seconds of cooking time. Stir in the basil.

2 Layer the cheese and salami slices on a plate, spreading some of the cheese mixture between each layer. Use remaining cream cheese mixture to spread on top and sides of loaf.

3 Sprinkle with parsley, pressing lightly to coat the cheese loaf. Chill cheese loaf for at least 3 hours; serve with assorted crackers.

Total Cooking Time: ½ to 1½ minutes

Parmesan-Bacon Cheese Log ▲

5 slices bacon
1 cup butter or margarine, cut into
   1-inch chunks
1 pkg. (8 oz.) cream cheese, cut into
   1-inch chunks
⅔ cup grated Parmesan cheese
3 tablespoons sliced green onions
⅛ teaspoon cayenne (optional)

10 to 12 servings

1 Arrange the bacon on a roasting rack; cover with a paper towel. Microwave at High for 3 to 7 minutes, or until the bacon is crisp and golden brown. Crumble bacon and set aside.

2 Combine the butter and cream cheese in a medium bowl. Microwave at 30% (Medium Low) for 1½ to 2½ minutes, or until mixture is softened, rotating bowl after every 30 seconds of cooking time. Add the crumbled bacon and remaining ingredients; mix well. Chill for 1 to 2 hours, or until the mixture firms slightly.

3 Wrap the cheese mixture in a sheet of plastic wrap and shape into a log. (If desired, unwrap and roll log in additional Parmesan cheese.) Chill wrapped cheese log for 2 to 3 hours; serve with assorted crackers or bread sticks.

Total Cooking Time: 4½ to 9½ minutes

Blue Cheese Log ▼

2 teaspoons butter or margarine
3 tablespoons sesame seed
1 pkg. (8 oz.) cream cheese
1 pkg. (4 oz.) blue cheese, crumbled
1 cup shredded Cheddar cheese
1 tablespoon sherry
1½ teaspoons Worcestershire sauce
¼ teaspoon onion powder
⅛ teaspoon garlic powder

10 to 12 servings

1 Melt the butter conventionally in a small skillet over medium heat. Add the sesame seed; stir constantly until the seed is light golden brown. Drain seed on paper towels; set aside.

2 Combine the cream cheese, blue cheese and the Cheddar cheese in a 2-quart casserole. Microwave at 50% (Medium) for 1 to 3 minutes, or until the cheeses are softened. Add remaining ingredients, except the sesame seed.

3 Beat the mixture at low speed of an electric mixer until fluffy. Chill cheese mixture for 1 to 2 hours, or until slightly firm.

4 Wrap the cheese mixture in a sheet of plastic wrap and shape into an 8-inch log. Unwrap the cheese log and roll evenly in the toasted sesame seed. Rewrap and chill cheese log for at least 2 more hours. Serve with assorted crackers.

Total Cooking Time: 1 to 3 minutes

Lentil Pâté ►

3 tablespoons butter or margarine
1 tablespoon dried parsley flakes
1 tablespoon instant minced onion
½ teaspoon instant chicken bouillon granules
⅛ teaspoon instant minced garlic
1 can (16 oz.) pinto beans, rinsed and drained
1 cup cooked lentils
1 tablespoon sherry
½ teaspoon salt
¼ teaspoon pepper

1½ cups

1 In a small bowl, combine the butter, parsley, onion, bouillon and garlic. Cover. Microwave at High for 1 to 1¼ minutes, or until butter melts.

2 Pour the butter mixture into a food processor or blender and add the remaining ingredients. Process until mixture is smooth.

3 Spoon the pâté mixture into a 2-cup crock or serving dish; cover and chill until firm. Serve pâté as a spread with crackers or garlic toast.

Total Cooking Time: 1 to 1¼ minutes

Frosted Pâté

1 lb. chicken livers, rinsed and drained
½ cup shredded carrot
¼ cup chopped onion
¼ cup butter or margarine
2 tablespoons sweet white wine
½ teaspoon salt
¼ teaspoon pepper
¼ teaspoon dry mustard
2 pkgs. (3 oz. each) cream cheese
1 tablespoon dried parsley flakes

2 cups

1 Cut a piece of wax paper to fit the bottom of a 2-cup mold. Butter the sides of the mold; set aside. In a 1-quart casserole, combine the chicken livers, carrot, onion, butter, wine, salt, pepper and mustard. Cover; microwave at High for 5 minutes, stirring once during cooking time.

2 Microwave at 50% (Medium) for 3 to 7 minutes longer, or until chicken livers are no longer pink, stirring once during cooking time.

3 Place mixture in a food processor or blender and process until smooth. Spoon the mixture into the prepared mold. Cover and chill for at least 4 hours. Unmold pâté onto a plate. Discard wax paper.

4 In a small bowl, microwave the cream cheese at 50% (Medium) for 1½ to 3 minutes, or until softened. Stir in the parsley.

5 Frost the top and sides of molded pâté with cream cheese mixture. Chill for 30 minutes to set; serve pâté with crackers, bread sticks or toasted French bread slices.

Total Cooking Time: 9½ to 15 minutes

Easy Chicken Pâté

1 lb. chicken livers, rinsed and drained
⅓ cup chopped fresh mushrooms
¼ cup butter or margarine, cut up
3 tablespoons chopped onion
2 tablespoons finely chopped celery
2 tablespoons dry vermouth
1 teaspoon instant chicken bouillon granules
½ teaspoon salt
¼ teaspoon dried rosemary leaves
⅛ teaspoon dried thyme leaves
⅛ teaspoon pepper
　Snipped fresh parsley (optional)

2 cups

1 Butter a 2-cup crock or serving dish; set aside. Combine all ingredients, except the parsley, in a 1½-quart casserole. Cover. Microwave at 70% (Medium High) for 11 to 15 minutes, or until the chicken livers are no longer pink, stirring 2 or 3 times during cooking.

2 Place mixture in a food processor or blender and process until smooth. Pour mixture into the prepared crock. Cover.

3 Chill pâté mixture for at least 6 hours, or overnight. Garnish with parsley, and serve with crackers, bread sticks or toasted French bread slices.

Total Cooking Time: 11 to 15 minutes

Pâté Tip:
For a more elegant presentation, spoon pâté mixture into a china or crystal bowl. Place the bowl in the center of your serving tray, and surround it with fancy cut vegetables, garlic toasts, and a variety of seasoned crackers or bread sticks.

Kabobs

Fancy, festive appetizers will add an exotic touch to any party

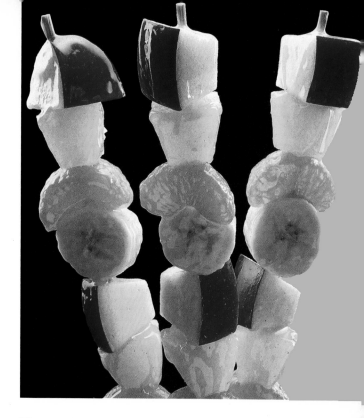

Treat yourself, your family or your friends to a truly unique taste experience in less than 10 minutes. Kabobs are easy and practical to prepare, and the results are always spectacular.

Peppered Chicken Kabobs

12 wooden skewers (6 inches long)
 1 whole boneless chicken breast (10 to 12 oz.) cut into 24 pieces, skin removed
 1 medium green pepper, cut into 24 chunks
 1 medium apple, cut into 24 chunks
 2 tablespoons vegetable oil
 1 teaspoon lemon juice
 1 teaspoon lemon pepper seasoning
 ¼ teaspoon salt

12 kabobs

1 Assemble each kabob by placing ingredients on a skewer in the following order: chicken, green pepper, apple, chicken, green pepper, apple. Repeat sequence to form 12 kabobs. Arrange kabobs on a roasting rack.

2 In a small bowl, combine the vegetable oil, lemon juice, lemon pepper and salt. Brush kabobs with the mixture; cover with wax paper.

3 Microwave kabobs at 50% (Medium) for 7 to 12 minutes, or until the chicken pieces are firm and no longer pink, rearranging the kabobs and brushing with lemon mixture once during cooking time.

Total Cooking Time: 7 to 12 minutes

Fruit Kabobs ▲

 6 wooden skewers (6 inches long)
Glaze:
 1 tablespoon cornstarch
 ⅛ teaspoon ground cinnamon
 ¼ cup lemon juice
 ¼ cup orange juice
 3 tablespoons honey

 1 medium apple, cut into 1-inch cubes
 1 can (8 oz.) pineapple chunks, drained
 1 can (11 oz.) mandarin orange segments, drained
 1 medium banana, cut into ½-inch slices

6 kabobs

1 Mix the cornstarch and cinnamon in a small bowl. Blend in the remaining glaze ingredients. Microwave at High for 1½ to 3½ minutes, or until mixture is clear and thickened, stirring once or twice during cooking time.

2 Assemble each kabob by placing ingredients on skewer in the following order: apple, pineapple, orange and banana. Alternate fruit until the skewer is filled; repeat to form 6 kabobs.

3 Brush kabobs with glaze; chill for 2 hours. Brush kabobs with glaze again before serving.

Total Cooking Time: 1½ to 3½ minutes

Seafood Kabobs

12 wooden picks (3 inches long)
 4 slices bacon, each cut into 3 pieces
 2 tablespoons soy sauce
 2 tablespoons honey
 2 tablespoons white wine
⅛ teaspoon garlic powder
12 whole water chestnuts
12 sea scallops (½ lb.)
 1 small green pepper, cut into 12 chunks

12 kabobs

Follow photo directions, below.

Total Cooking Time: 6¾ to 9½ minutes

How to Microwave Seafood Kabobs

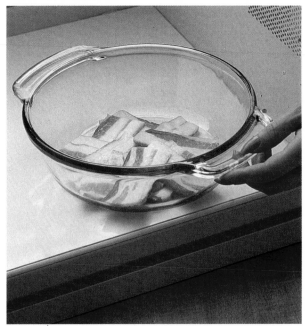

1 In a 1-quart casserole, microwave the bacon pieces at High for 1 to 1½ minutes, or just until bacon begins to brown. Drain, reserving 1 tablespoon of bacon drippings in the casserole. Set bacon aside on a paper-towel-lined plate.

2 Add the soy sauce, honey, wine and garlic powder to the casserole; stir. Microwave at High for 45 seconds to 1 minute, or until the marinade mixture can be stirred smooth. Set aside.

3 Wrap 1 piece of bacon around each water chestnut. Assemble each kabob by placing ingredients on skewer in the following order: scallop, bacon-wrapped water chestnut, and green pepper chunk. Repeat to form 12 kabobs.

4 Place kabobs in marinade mixture; turn to coat. Cover and chill for 1 to 2 hours. Arrange the kabobs on a roasting rack with the scallops toward the outside.

5 Microwave at 50% (Medium) for 5 to 7 minutes, or until the scallops are firm and opaque, turning kabobs over and basting with marinade once during cooking time.

Apricot-Sausage Kabobs ▲

30 wooden picks (3 inches long)
 1 pkg. (8 oz.) fully cooked sausage links
 1 can (16 oz.) apricot halves, drained
    (reserve ¾ cup juice)
¼ cup soy sauce
 2 tablespoons packed brown sugar
 1 can (15½ oz.) pineapple chunks, drained

                                          30 kabobs

1 Cut each sausage link into 3 pieces. Set aside. Combine the reserved apricot juice, soy sauce and brown sugar in a small bowl. Stir in the sausage pieces; let stand for 5 minutes. Cut each apricot half into 2 pieces. Drain the sausages, reserving the sauce.

2 Assemble each kabob by placing ingredients on a pick in the following order: apricot, sausage and pineapple. Repeat sequence to form 30 kabobs.

3 Arrange 15 kabobs on a roasting rack; brush with reserved sauce. Microwave the kabobs at High for 3 to 5 minutes, or until hot, turning over and basting with sauce once during cooking time. Repeat with remaining kabobs.

Total Cooking Time: 6 to 10 minutes

Vegetable Kabobs with Lemon Dressing ➤

 8 wooden skewers (6 inches long)
Lemon Dressing:
 3 tablespoons butter or margarine
 1 tablespoon lemon juice
¼ teaspoon onion powder
⅛ teaspoon dried marjoram leaves
    Dash pepper
 8 frozen Brussels sprouts
 8 frozen baby carrots
 1 small green pepper, cut into 16 chunks
 8 fresh cauliflowerets (1-inch pieces)
 2 tablespoons water

                                          8 kabobs

1 In a 1-cup measure, microwave butter at High for 1 to 1¼ minutes, or until melted. Add the remaining dressing ingredients. Set aside.

2 Combine the Brussels sprouts and carrots in a 1-quart casserole. Cover; microwave at High for 1½ to 3 minutes, or until vegetables are defrosted. Let vegetables stand for 5 minutes.

3 Assemble each kabob by placing vegetable pieces on skewer in the following order: Brussels sprout, carrot, green pepper chunk, caulifloweret and another green pepper chunk. Repeat sequence to form 8 kabobs.

4 Arrange kabobs on a plate, with the Brussels sprouts toward center of dish. Sprinkle kabobs with water; cover with plastic wrap.

5 Microwave kabobs at High for 3 to 5 minutes, or until the vegetables are tender-crisp, rotating plate once during cooking time. Let stand, covered, for 3 to 4 minutes. Pour dressing over kabobs to serve.

Total Cooking Time: 5½ to 9¼ minutes

Kabob Tip:
For best results, leave a small amount of space between ingredients as you place them on the skewers. Kabobs packed too tightly will not microwave as evenly or quickly.

Turkey Melon Kabobs ➤

14 to 16 wooden picks (3 inches long)
¼ cup apricot jam
1 tablespoon teriyaki sauce
1 teaspoon honey
⅛ teaspoon salt
⅛ teaspoon ground cinnamon
⅛ teaspoon sesame oil (optional)
1 turkey tenderloin (about ½ lb.) cut into
    1-inch cubes
14 to 16 cantaloupe or honeydew melon balls

14 to 16 kabobs

1 In a small bowl, blend the jam, teriyaki sauce, honey, salt, cinnamon and sesame oil. Add the cubed turkey and stir to coat. Cover; chill mixture for at least 2 hours.

2 Assemble each kabob by placing 1 turkey cube and 1 melon ball on a wooden pick. Repeat with remaining turkey and melon pieces. Arrange kabobs on a roasting rack.

3 Microwave kabobs at 70% (Medium High) for 3½ to 6 minutes, or until the turkey is firm and no longer pink, rotating rack twice during cooking time.

Total Cooking Time: 3½ to 6 minutes

Greek Kabobs ▲

6 wooden skewers (6 inches long)
3 thin slices lemon (optional)
2 tablespoons olive or vegetable oil
¼ teaspoon garlic powder
¾ lb. boneless lamb shoulder, cut into
    12 pieces
1 small onion, quartered and separated
6 pitted black olives
6 cherry tomatoes

6 kabobs

1 Combine the lemon slices, olive oil and garlic powder in a small bowl. Microwave at High for 30 seconds to 1 minute, or until mixture is hot. Add the lamb cubes; stir to coat. Cover and chill for 1 hour.

2 Assemble each kabob by placing ingredients on a skewer in the following order: onion piece, black olive, lamb cube, cherry tomato, lamb cube, olive and onion piece. (If desired, lemon slices from marinade may be reserved and placed on kabobs.) Repeat sequence to form 6 kabobs.

3 Arrange kabobs on a roasting rack; cover with wax paper. Microwave at 50% (Medium) for 5 to 8 minutes, or until the lamb reaches desired doneness, rotating rack and turning kabobs over once during cooking time.

Total Cooking Time: 5½ to 9 minutes

Sunny Turkey Roll-ups ▲

12 wooden picks (3 inches long)
 2 turkey cutlets (2 to 3 oz. each) ¼ inch thick

Marinade:

⅓ cup orange juice
 2 teaspoons packed brown sugar
 1 teaspoon vinegar
 ¼ teaspoon salt
 ¼ teaspoon ground ginger

Glaze:

 2 tablespoons orange marmalade
 ½ teaspoon prepared mustard

 6 frozen baby carrots

12 appetizers

1 Cut the turkey cutlets into 12 strips, about
 3½ × ¾ inches; set aside. Combine the marinade ingredients in a small bowl; mix well.

Microwave at High for 30 seconds to 1 minute,
or until the mixture is hot. Stir; let mixture cool
slightly. Stir in the turkey strips. Cover; chill for
4 to 6 hours.

2 Remove turkey strips from marinade. Reserve
 1 teaspoon of the marinade in a small bowl
and add the glaze ingredients. Mix well.

3 Cut each carrot in half crosswise. Wrap 1
 turkey strip around each carrot piece; secure
with wooden picks. Brush roll-ups with glaze.

4 Arrange roll-ups in a circular pattern in a
 9-inch round baking dish. Microwave at High
for 2 to 4 minutes, or until the turkey is no
longer pink, rotating dish once or twice during
cooking time.

Total Cooking Time: 2½ to 5 minutes

Vegetable Appetizers

The best of all worlds:
taste, texture, color & nutrition

◄ Seasoned Vegie Combo Tray

2 medium carrots, sliced diagonally
2 cups fresh broccoli flowerets
2 cups fresh cauliflowerets
¼ lb. peeled and seeded acorn squash, cut into
  1-inch chunks
1 small zucchini, thinly sliced
2 tablespoons water
1 small tomato, cut into 8 wedges
2 tablespoons butter or margarine
1 tablespoon grated Parmesan cheese
½ teaspoon onion salt

6 to 8 servings

1 On a 10-inch plate, arrange the vegetables in a circular pattern in the following order: Arrange carrots around the outside edge. Arrange broccoli and cauliflowerets, placing pieces end-to-end. Arrange squash next, with chunks overlapping the broccoli and cauliflower. Arrange zucchini pieces in the center.

2 Sprinkle vegetables with the water. Cover with plastic wrap; microwave at High for 6 to 8 minutes, or until the vegetables are fork-tender, rotating plate twice during cooking time.

3 Arrange the tomato wedges over vegetables. Re-cover; microwave at High for 1 to 2 minutes, or until the tomatoes are hot. Drain; set aside.

4 In a 1-cup measure, microwave the butter at High for 45 seconds to 1 minute, or until melted. Stir in the Parmesan cheese and onion salt. Pour mixture over the vegetables; serve with wooden picks.

Total Cooking Time: 7¾ to 11 minutes

Marinated Vegetables ▲

1 cup thinly sliced carrots
1 cup fresh broccoli flowerets
1 cup fresh cauliflowerets
½ cup green pepper chunks
1 small onion, thinly sliced
¼ cup water
⅛ teaspoon garlic powder
8 oz. fresh mushrooms, cut in half
⅔ cup vinegar
½ cup vegetable oil
2 teaspoons salt
2 teaspoons dried basil leaves
1½ teaspoons sugar
¼ teaspoon pepper

6 to 8 servings

1 In a 2-quart casserole, combine the carrots, broccoli, cauliflower, green pepper, onion, water and garlic powder. Cover; microwave at High for 4 to 5 minutes, or just until the colors of vegetables brighten, stirring once during cooking time. Stir in the mushrooms; set aside.

2 Blend all the remaining ingredients in a small bowl. Pour mixture over the vegetables; stir gently. Chill vegetables for at least 8 hours, stirring occasionally. Serve with wooden picks.

Total Cooking Time: 4 to 5 minutes

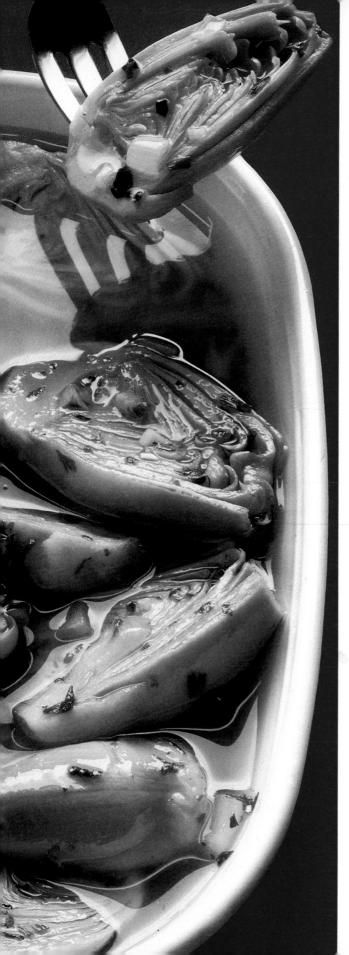

◄ Artichokes Vinaigrette

   2 pkgs. (9 oz. each) frozen artichoke hearts
 ⅔ cup olive or vegetable oil
 ¼ cup white wine vinegar
   2 tablespoons chopped onion
   1 teaspoon sugar
 ½ teaspoon dried parsley flakes
 ¼ teaspoon grated lemon peel
 ¼ teaspoon garlic powder
 ⅛ teaspoon dried tarragon leaves

6 to 8 servings

1 Unwrap the artichoke hearts and place in a 2-quart casserole. Cover; microwave at High for 8 to 9 minutes, or until artichoke hearts are defrosted, stirring to break apart once during cooking time. Drain; set aside.

2 Combine the remaining ingredients in a 2-cup measure. Microwave at High for 1 to 1½ minutes, or until mixture is hot.

3 Pour hot mixture over artichoke hearts; cover. Chill for at least 8 hours; serve artichokes with wooden picks.

Total Cooking Time: 9 to 10½ minutes

Variation:

Vegetables Vinaigrette:
Follow recipe for Artichokes Vinaigrette, except: substitute 1 pkg. (10 oz.) frozen cauliflowerets for the artichokes; cut 1 medium tomato into wedges and stir wedges into vegetable mixture 1 hour before serving.

Time-saving Tip:
Prepare Vegetables Vinaigrette 1 day in advance for your next party. You'll save time, and the vegetables will intensify in flavor. Be inventive: create different color combinations by choosing different vegetables.

Pickled Mushrooms

12 oz. fresh mushrooms
1 small onion, thinly sliced
1 small green pepper, cut into thin strips
½ cup white wine vinegar
¼ cup chopped pimiento-stuffed olives
3 tablespoons olive or vegetable oil
1 teaspoon dried parsley flakes
½ teaspoon sugar
½ teaspoon salt
¼ teaspoon pepper
⅛ teaspoon instant minced garlic
⅛ teaspoon dried thyme leaves

6 servings

1 Combine all ingredients in a 2-quart casserole. Cover; microwave at High for 3 to 5 minutes, or until the mixture is hot, stirring once during cooking time.

2 Chill mushrooms for at least 4 hours. Drain; serve pickled mushrooms with wooden picks.

Total Cooking Time: 3 to 5 minutes

Stuffed Celery ▲

3 tablespoons water
2 tablespoons dried vegetable flakes
½ teaspoon dried onion flakes
1 pkg. (3 oz.) cream cheese
4 celery stalks
Paprika

20 appetizers

1 Combine the water, vegetable flakes and onion flakes in a 1-cup measure. Cover with plastic wrap. Microwave at High for 30 to 45 seconds, or until flakes are tender. Set aside.

2 In a small bowl, microwave the cream cheese at High for 15 to 30 seconds, or until softened. Stir in the vegetable flake mixture.

3 Stuff the celery stalks with the vegetable-cheese mixture. Cut each stalk into 5 pieces; sprinkle with paprika before serving.

Total Cooking Time: ¾ to 1¼ minutes

◄ Stuffed Mushrooms

Classic Stuffed Mushrooms

- 18 fresh mushrooms (8 oz.)
- ¼ cup finely chopped onion
- 2 tablespoons butter or margarine
- ⅓ cup seasoned dry bread crumbs
- 1½ teaspoons dried parsley flakes
- ¼ teaspoon salt
- ⅛ teaspoon garlic powder

18 appetizers

Follow photo directions, below.

Cheese & Walnut Stuffed Mushrooms

- 18 fresh mushrooms (8 oz.)
- ⅓ cup chopped walnuts
- 2 oz. blue cheese, crumbled
- 3 tablespoons seasoned dry bread crumbs

18 appetizers

Follow photo directions, below.

How to Microwave Stuffed Mushrooms

1 Remove stems from the mushrooms. Set mushroom caps aside. Chop the mushroom stems; place the chopped stems (combined with onion and butter, if included in recipe) in a 1-quart casserole. Cover.

Ham & Cheese Stuffed Mushrooms

1 pkg. (3 oz.) cream cheese
18 fresh mushrooms (8 oz.)
1 tablespoon butter or margarine
½ cup finely chopped fully cooked ham
¼ cup finely chopped almonds

18 appetizers

Microwave cream cheese at High for 15 to 30 seconds, or until softened. Continue with photo directions, below.

Smoked Cheese & Salami Mushrooms

18 fresh mushrooms (8 oz.)
2 tablespoons finely chopped onion
¼ cup pasteurized process smoked
    cheese spread
¼ cup seasoned dry bread crumbs
¼ cup finely chopped salami

18 appetizers

Follow photo directions, below.

Spinach-stuffed Mushrooms

1 pkg. (12 oz.) frozen spinach soufflé
18 fresh mushrooms (8 oz.)
¼ cup shredded Cheddar cheese
¼ cup seasoned dry bread crumbs
¼ teaspoon dried thyme leaves

18 appetizers

Unwrap the frozen soufflé. Cut soufflé in half. Rewrap one half and return to freezer for later use; place the remaining soufflé in a 1-quart casserole. Cover; microwave at 50% (Medium) for 2 to 4 minutes, or until soufflé is defrosted, stirring once during cooking time. Continue with photo directions, below.

Total Cooking Time: 3 to 10 minutes

2 Microwave at High for 1½ to 2½ minutes, or until chopped mushrooms are tender. Stir in the other stuffing ingredients. Arrange the mushroom caps on a paper-towel-lined plate.

3 Spoon the mixture into the mushroom caps. Microwave stuffed mushrooms at High for 1½ to 3½ minutes, or until hot, rotating plate once or twice during cooking time.

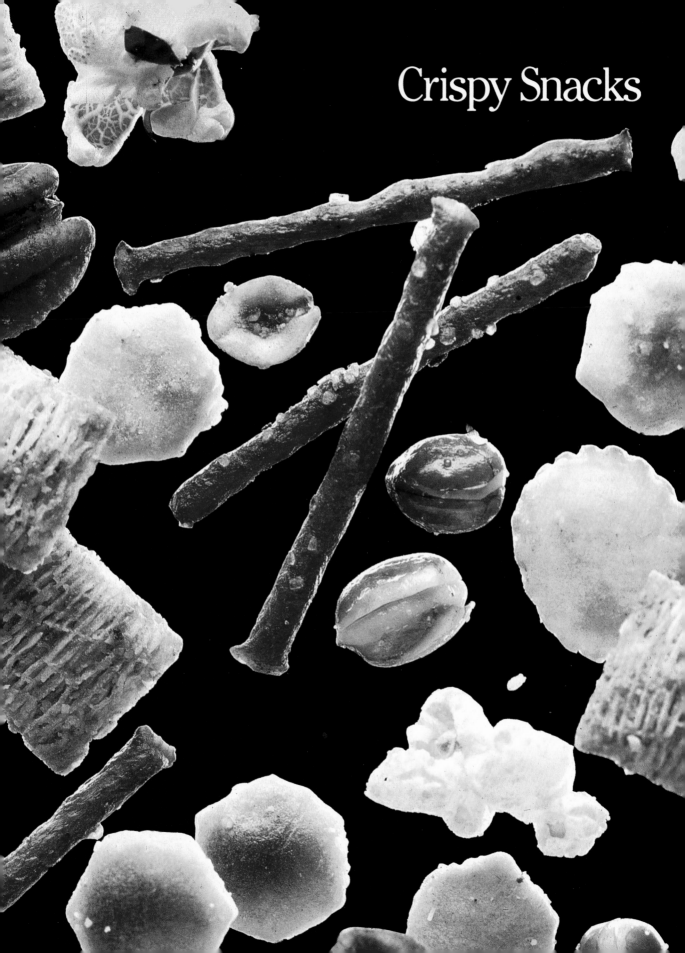

Crispy Snacks

Crispy Snacks

A dozen traditional treats for make-ahead party planning or spur-of-the-moment enjoyment

◄ Cheese Popcorn

8 cups popped popcorn
¼ cup plus 2 tablespoons butter or margarine
¼ cup grated American cheese food
¼ cup grated Parmesan cheese
    Seasoned salt

8 cups

Place the popcorn in a large bowl; set aside. In a 2-cup measure, microwave the butter at High for 1½ to 1¾ minutes, or until melted. Stir in the cheeses; drizzle mixture over popcorn and toss to coat. Sprinkle with seasoned salt to taste.

Total Cooking Time: 1½ to 1¾ minutes

How to Microwave Popcorn

Microwave popcorn only in a popper designed specifically for the microwave. *Do not* microwave popcorn in a paper bag; it may catch fire. Follow manufacturer's instructions for amounts and cooking times: be careful not to overcook.

Savory Snack Mix ▲

3 cups thin pretzel sticks
1 cup Spanish peanuts
2 tablespoons butter or margarine
2 teaspoons Worcestershire sauce
½ teaspoon chili powder
¼ teaspoon red pepper sauce
⅛ teaspoon garlic salt

4 cups

1 Combine the pretzels and peanuts in a 2-quart casserole; set aside. In a 1-cup measure, combine the remaining ingredients. Microwave at High for 45 seconds to 1 minute, or until butter melts. Stir.

2 Pour butter mixture over pretzels and peanuts, tossing to coat. Microwave at High for 3 to 5 minutes, or until mixture is hot and the butter is absorbed, stirring 2 or 3 times during cooking. Spread snack mix on a paper-towel-lined baking sheet to cool. Store in airtight containers.

Total Cooking Time: 3¾ to 6 minutes

Piquant Pecans ▲

¼ cup plus 2 tablespoons butter or margarine
2 tablespoons steak sauce
1 teaspoon soy sauce
¼ teaspoon red pepper sauce
1 lb. pecan halves

4 cups

1 In a 2-quart casserole, microwave butter at High for 1¼ to 1½ minutes, or until melted.

2 Blend the sauces into the melted butter. Add the pecans and stir to coat. Microwave at High for 7 to 13 minutes, or until the pecans are hot.

3 Spread pecans on a paper-towel-lined baking sheet to cool. Store in airtight containers.

Total Cooking Time: 8¼ to 14½ minutes

Cheese Nuggets

½ cup butter or margarine
1 cup dry-roasted peanuts (optional)
½ cup grated Parmesan cheese
1 teaspoon Worcestershire sauce
⅛ teaspoon cayenne (optional)
4 cups bite-size shredded wheat cereal

4 to 5 cups

1 In a 2-quart casserole, microwave the butter at High for 1½ to 1¾ minutes, or until melted. Stir in peanuts, Parmesan cheese, Worcestershire sauce and cayenne. Add the wheat cereal, stirring to coat.

2 Microwave at 50% (Medium) for 5 to 7 minutes, or until the mixture browns slightly, stirring 2 or 3 times during cooking. Spread mixture on a paper-towel-lined baking sheet to cool. Store in airtight containers.

Total Cooking Time: 6½ to 8¾ minutes

Cheesy Snackers

1 cup butter or margarine
1½ teaspoons celery salt
½ teaspoon onion powder
¼ teaspoon garlic powder
5 to 6 cups oyster crackers
½ cup grated Parmesan cheese

5 to 6 cups

1 In a large bowl, microwave the butter at High for 2 to 2½ minutes, or until melted. Stir in the celery salt, onion powder and garlic powder. Add the crackers, stirring to coat, then mix in the Parmesan cheese.

2 Pour mixture onto a baking sheet. Allow the mixture to cool completely. Store in airtight containers.

Total Cooking Time: 2 to 2½ minutes

Hot & Spicy Roasted Peanuts ▲

1 cup shelled raw peanuts
1 teaspoon vegetable oil
¼ to ½ teaspoon seasoned salt
⅛ teaspoon cayenne (optional)

1 cup

Combine all the ingredients in a 9-inch pie plate; toss with a fork to coat. Microwave at High for 5 to 7 minutes, or just until the nuts begin to turn light brown, stirring after the first 2 minutes and then after every minute of cooking time.

Total Cooking Time: 5 to 7 minutes

Corn & Nut Clusters

- 8 cups popped popcorn
- 1½ cups dry-roasted peanuts
- 1¼ cups sugar
- 1 cup butter or margarine
- ½ cup light corn syrup
- 1 teaspoon vanilla

10 cups

1 Combine the popcorn and peanuts in a large greased bowl; set aside. Line a baking sheet with wax paper. Set aside.

2 In an 8-cup measure, combine the sugar, butter and corn syrup. Insert a microwave candy thermometer.

3 Microwave at High for 11 to 19 minutes, or until thermometer registers 310°F (Hard Crack Stage, right). Stir mixture every 3 minutes during cooking time.

4 Stir the vanilla into the hot syrup; pour over the popcorn mixture. Stir until popcorn is well coated. Spread the mixture into a single layer on the prepared baking sheet and let stand until cool. Break hardened mixture into pieces and store in airtight containers.

Total Cooking Time: 11 to 19 minutes

Caramel Corn ▲

- 5 cups popped popcorn
- 3 tablespoons butter or margarine
- ¾ cup packed brown sugar
- ⅓ cup raw peanuts
- 3 tablespoons dark corn syrup
- ½ teaspoon vanilla
- ¼ teaspoon baking soda
  Dash salt

5 cups

Place the popcorn in a large greased bowl; set aside. Line a baking sheet with wax paper; set aside. Continue with photo directions, right.

Total Cooking Time: 5½ to 8¾ minutes

How to Test Candy for Doneness:
If you don't have a microwave-safe thermometer, use cold water test to judge doneness. Fill a cup with very cold water; drop about ½ teaspoon of mixture into the cup. Let stand for a few seconds, then test syrup with your fingers.

Soft Crack Stage: Syrup separates into hard *but not* brittle threads.
Hard Crack Stage: Syrup separates into hard *and* brittle threads.

How to Microwave Caramel Corn

1 In an 8-cup measure, microwave the butter at High for 1 to 1¼ minutes, or until melted. Stir in the brown sugar, peanuts and corn syrup. Insert a microwave candy thermometer.

2 Microwave at High for 3 to 6 minutes, or until the mixture reaches 280°F (Soft Crack Stage, opposite). Mix in the remaining ingredients.

3 Pour the hot syrup mixture over the popcorn, stirring to coat. Microwave at High for 1½ minutes, stirring once during cooking time and again after cooking is completed.

4 Spread mixture on the prepared baking sheet. Let stand until cool; break mixture into pieces and store in airtight containers.

Home-made Granola

1½ cups uncooked old-fashioned rolled oats
  ¼ cup flaked coconut
  ¼ cup sliced almonds
  ⅓ cup honey
  2 tablespoons packed brown sugar
  2 tablespoons vegetable oil
  1 teaspoon molasses

  ½ teaspoon ground cinnamon
  ½ teaspoon vanilla
  ¼ cup raisins (optional)
  ¼ cup chopped dried apples (optional)

3 cups

Follow photo directions, below.

Total Cooking Time: 5½ to 9½ minutes

How to Microwave Home-made Granola

1 Combine the oats, coconut and almonds in a medium bowl; set aside. Line a baking sheet with wax paper; set aside.

2 In an 8-cup measure, combine remaining ingredients, except raisins and apples. Microwave at High for 1½ to 2½ minutes, or until mixture boils, stirring once during cooking time.

3 Pour the honey mixture over the oats, tossing to coat. Microwave at High for 4 to 7 minutes, or until the mixture appears dry and begins to stiffen, stirring 2 or 3 times during cooking.

4 Stir in raisins and apples. Spread mixture on prepared baking sheet and let cool. Break into pieces and store in airtight containers.

Granola Bars (pictured on page 90)

¼ cup butter or margarine
¼ cup packed brown sugar
1 large egg
¼ teaspoon almond extract
⅛ teaspoon salt
3 cups prepared Home-made Granola, without
  raisins (page 91)

8 bars

1 In a small bowl, microwave the butter at High
for 1¼ to 1½ minutes, or until melted. Set aside.
In a medium bowl, combine the sugar, egg,
almond extract and salt.

2 Add the melted butter to the sugar mixture,
stirring to combine. Add the granola, stirring to
coat. Press mixture into a greased 9-inch square
baking dish.

3 Microwave at High for 6 to 8 minutes, or until
the mixture is firm to the touch, rotating dish
after first 2 minutes, and then after every minute of
cooking time. (Bars may appear slightly wet on
top, but will feel firm to the touch.) Let stand until
completely cool; cut into 8 bars.

Total Cooking Time: 7¼ to 9½ minutes

Granola Snacks ▲

½ cup packed brown sugar
⅓ cup butter or margarine
3 tablespoons honey
2 tablespoons water
½ teaspoon salt
½ teaspoon ground cinnamon
2 cups uncooked old-fashioned rolled oats
⅔ cup sunflower nuts or sliced almonds
⅔ cup wheat germ
⅔ cup flaked coconut

1 lb.

1 Grease a baking sheet; set aside. In a 2-quart
casserole, combine the sugar, butter, honey,
water, salt and cinnamon. Microwave at High for
6 to 9 minutes, or until the mixture is slightly
thickened and blended, stirring 2 or 3 times
during cooking.

2 Add the remaining ingredients; stir to coat.
Microwave at 50% (Medium) for 6 to 9
minutes, or until the mixture turns golden
brown, stirring 2 or 3 times during cooking.

3 Spread the mixture on prepared baking sheet.
Press lightly with a spatula to flatten; let stand
until cool. Break granola into pieces and store in
airtight containers.

Total Cooking Time: 12 to 18 minutes

Caramel Apples ►

6 wooden Popsicle sticks
6 firm tart apples
1 pkg. (14 oz.) caramels
2 tablespoons half-and-half
¼ cup chocolate-flavored candy sprinkles

6 servings

1 Line a baking sheet with wax paper; set aside.
Insert a Popsicle stick in the stem end of each
apple. Set aside. Place caramels and half-and-
half in a 2-quart casserole. Microwave at High for
3 to 4 minutes, or until caramels melt, stirring after
every minute of cooking time.

2 Dip each apple in hot caramel, turning to coat.
Coat bottoms of apples with candy sprinkles.
Arrange apples on prepared baking sheet; let
stand until caramel is cooled and set.

Total Cooking Time: 3 to 4 minutes

INDEX

CY DE COSSE INCORPORATED
Chairman: Cy DeCosse
President: James B. Maus
Executive Vice President: William B. Jones

CREDITS
Design, Production & Photography:
  Cy DeCosse Incorporated
Art Directors: Bill Nelson, Bill Jones
Project Manager: Lynette Reber
Home Economists: Peggy Lamb, Jill Crum,
  Kathy Weber
Production Manager: Jim Bindas
Assistant Production Manager: Julie Churchill
Copy Editor: Bryan Trandem
Typesetting: Jennie Smith, Linda Schloegel
Production Staff: Michelle Joy, Yelena
  Konrardy, Lisa Rosenthal, David
  Schelitzche, Cathleen Shannon, Nik
  Wogstad
Photographers: Rex Irmen, Tony Kubat,
  John Lauenstein, Mette Nielsen
Food Stylists: Teresa Ernst, Susan Sinon,
  Suzanne Finley, Robin Krause,
  Susan Zechmann
Production Consultant: Christine Watkins
Special Microwave Consultant:
  Barbara Methven
Color Separations: La Cromolito
Printing: R.R. Donnelley & Sons (1186)